T0089165

Cambridge Elements ≡

Elements in Publishing and Book Culture
edited by
Samantha Rayner
University College London
Leah Tether
University of Bristol

SIMULATING ANTIQUITY IN BOYS' ADVENTURE FICTION

Maps and Ink Stains

Thomas Vranken
University of the South Pacific

CAMBRIDGE UNIVERSITY PRESS

CAMBRIDGE
UNIVERSITY PRESS

University Printing House, Cambridge CB2 8BS, United Kingdom

One Liberty Plaza, 20th Floor, New York, NY 10006, USA

477 Williamstown Road, Port Melbourne, VIC 3207, Australia

314–321, 3rd Floor, Plot 3, Splendor Forum, Jasola District Centre,
New Delhi – 110025, India

103 Penang Road, #05–06/07, Visioncrest Commercial, Singapore 238467

Cambridge University Press is part of the University of Cambridge.

It furthers the University's mission by disseminating knowledge in the pursuit of
education, learning, and research at the highest international levels of excellence.

www.cambridge.org
Information on this title: www.cambridge.org/9781009158947
DOI: 10.1017/9781009158930

© Thomas Vranken 2022

First published 2022

A catalogue record for this publication is available from the British Library.

ISBN 978-1-009-15894-7 Paperback
ISSN 2514-8524 (online)
ISSN 2514-8516 (print)

Simulating Antiquity in Boys' Adventure Fiction
Maps and Ink Stains

Elements in Publishing and Book Culture

DOI: 10.1017/9781009158930
First published online: August 2022

Thomas Vranken
University of the South Pacific

Author for correspondence: Thomas Vranken, thomas.vranken@usp.ac.fj

ABSTRACT: A genre that glorifies brutish masculinity and late Victorian imperialism, boys' 'lost world' adventure fiction has traditionally been studied for its politically problematic content. While attuned to these concerns, this Element approaches the genre from a different angle, viewing adventure fiction as not just a catalogue of texts but a corpus of books. Examining early editions of *Treasure Island*, *King Solomon's Mines*, and *The Lost World*, the Element argues that *fin-de-siècle* adventure fiction sought to resist the nineteenth-century industrialisation of book production from within. As the Element points out, the genre is filled with nostalgic simulations of material anachronisms – 'facsimiles' of fictional pre-modern paper, printing, and handwriting that re-humanise the otherwise alienating landscape of the modern book and modern literary production. The Element ends by exploring a subversive revival of lost world adventure fiction that emerged in response to e-books at the beginning of the twenty-first century.

KEYWORDS: adventure fiction, automation, simulation, obsolescence and nostalgia, literary maps

ISBNs: 9781009158947 (PB), 9781009158930 (OC)
ISSNs: 2514-8524 (online), 2514-8516 (print)

Contents

If . . . all the old romance, retold
Exactly in the ancient way,
Can please, as me they pleased of old,
The wiser youngsters of today . . .

   R. L. Stevenson, *'To the Hesitating Purchaser'*, Treasure Island
   (1883)

Introduction

The nineteenth-century industrialisation of book production has traditionally been framed as a process of linear supersedence. Over the course of the
nineteenth century, this narrative asserts, hand presses were replaced by
steam presses, handwriting was replaced by typewriting, manual typesetting
was replaced by composing machines, the quotidian rags used to make
paper were replaced by first esparto grass and then wood pulp, and vatmen
were replaced by Fourdrinier conveyor-belt machines (see, for instance,
Clair; Fyfe). To quote John Feather:

> The printing process at the beginning of the nineteenth
> century was essentially unchanged from the methods which
> Gutenberg had invented 350 years before. Typesetting, print-
> ing and binding were all handcraft processes, as were paper-
> making and typefounding. Within a hundred years this was
> transformed. (p. 86)

As Alexander Starre points out, however, while 'processes of obsolescence
can seem like a one-way street, with discarded commodities, technologies,
or media falling away from everyday use', 'objects that have become
outmoded and obsolete may persist or resurface in different products and
with different cultural values' (p. 128). And, indeed, at the time, the
illustrator Henry Blackburn observed that

> the nineteenth-century author's love for the literature of his
> past has led him to imitate not only the style, but the outward
> appearance of old books; and by a series of frauds (to which
> his publisher has lent himself only too readily) to produce
> something which appears to be what it is not. (p. 204)

This Element explores this notion of the bibliographic 'fraud' and the
ways in which authors and their bookmaking associates worked together
to create what I am calling 'simulations of antiquity' within the thoroughly industrialised sphere of late Victorian publishing. In so doing,

the Element will avoid the well-trodden scholarly path that tours William Morris and the high-end, limited edition, artisan creations of the Kelmscott Press, and turn instead to open up a still relatively uncut trail leading to the more economically accessible world of boys' 'lost world' adventure fiction.

William S. Peterson has noted that the Kelmscott Press was 'merely the most visible manifestation' of late Victorian publishing's broader antiquarian impulse (p. 26), and, while the antiquarian aspects of adventure fiction are less overt than those of the Kelmscott Press, the genre itself was also more pervasive. In today's money, the Kelmscott Press charged between a couple of hundred and a couple of thousand pounds for each of the books that it created. As a result, each of these books sold only a few hundred copies. The five shillings required to buy an early edition of an adventure fiction novel, on the other hand, amount to just over sixteen pounds today, allowing each of these novels to reach thousands or even tens of thousands of buying readers in their first year alone.[1] For, while Morris (and his counterparts at other small antiquarian presses) chose largely to opt out of modern commercial book production, parts of Victorian adventure fiction, I suggest, enacted a conceptually richer resistance to industrial publishing from within, in a nostalgic personal and civilisational return to childhood. While drafting *Treasure Island*, in the second half of 1881, Robert Louis Stevenson and his thirteen-year-old stepson Lloyd Osbourne, for whom *Treasure Island* was initially written,[2] were also thoroughly ensconced in experiments with a small hand press. Together, Stevenson and Osbourne

---

[1] Five shillings was, for instance, the initial price of two of the novels discussed in this Element, *Treasure Island* (1883) and *King Solomon's Mines* (1885). For these prices, see the following advertisements: 'Treasure Island. A Story of the Spanish Main'; 'King Solomon's Mines. A Thrilling Tale Founded on an African Legend'. According to the National Archives' online historical currency converter tool, five shillings in 1880 equates to £16.55 today ('Currency Converter: 1270–2017'). By contrast, advertisements for the Kelmscott Press show that their books sold for between £2 and £25 ('Mr. William Morris's Kelmscott Press Publications'), the equivalent of between £164 and £2,051 today. For the sales figures referenced in this Element's Chronology, see Garside, p. 260.
[2] See Stevenson, 'To W. E. Henley'; Stevenson, 'My First Book'.

would compose short comic poems, stories, and colophons, carve wood-block engravings, set type, and then manually print their creations (for a first-hand account of these activities, see Japp, p. 15). 'The Author and the printer', declares the colophon to one such pamphlet,

> With various kinds of skill
> Concocted it in Winter
> At Davos on the Hill.
> They burned the nightly taper
> But now the work is ripe,
> Observe the costly paper,
> Remark the perfect type! (Stevenson and Osbourne, p. 8).

Alastair Bonnett has recently shown how the word 'nostalgia' (counter-intuitively, that most modern of emotions) only began shifting towards its current meaning in the late nineteenth century (p. 2); and, paradoxically, the toy hand press that Stevenson and his stepson used to print these pamphlets was itself an industrially mass-produced commodity (see Hart, pp. 1–5). The same desire to revive a pre-industrial mode of print culture within industrial print culture informs, I suggest, a broader strain of late Victorian adventure fiction.

As well as *Treasure Island* itself, the first three sections of this Element focus on H. Rider Haggard's *King Solomon's Mines* (1885), and Arthur Conan Doyle's *The Lost World* (1912).[3] Taken together, these novels

---

[3] Each of these novels directly inspired the creation of the next. In his autobio-graphy, Haggard claims that he began writing *King Solomon's Mines* after he 'read in one of the weekly papers a notice of Stevenson's "Treasure Island" so laudatory that I procured and studied that work, and was impelled by its perusal to try to write a book for boys' (p. 220). In 1889, Doyle told his mother that he was 'thinking of writing a Rider-Haggardy kind of book . . . dedicated to all the naughty boys of the Empire' (cited in Lellenberg *et al.* pp. 577); starting on the project would take him twenty years, but *The Lost World* explicitly (if also somewhat competitively) acknowledges its debt to *King Solomon's Mines* when, in preparing for the novel's main battle, Lord John Roxton declares 'The "Last

represent three cornerstones of a *fin-de-siècle* literary movement Michael Saler terms the 'New Romance': a highly paratextual genre, dense with imaginary maps, photographs, footnotes, appendices, 'facsimiles' of hand-writing, and character-drawn illustrations. For Saler, a socio-historian, the New Romance produced 'spectacular texts' that were designed to 're-enchant' an otherwise disenchanted Weberian world of all-explaining scientific rationalism (pp. 57–104). As a materially inclined literary scholar, I view the New Romance as not just a sociological movement but also a materio-literary movement – a movement working to make modern books and modern authorship seem old again by resurrecting a simulacrum of pre-industrial papermaking (Section 1), printing (Section 2), and handwriting (Section 3), within what remained a distinctly industrial mass medium. At the end of his study of the rag-paper era in the United States, Jonathan Senchyne casts the nineteenth-century mechanisation of book production as fundamentally 'alienating' and de-humanising (p. 158). In this Element, I argue that New Romance adventure fiction sought to ameliorate this sense of alienating rupture, re-imbuing industrial books with the human intimacy of their pre-industrial predecessors. In the process, these books become both commodities and *anti*-commodities, concealing as they do not the human labour on which they rely (à la Marx's commodity fetishism) but the automated mechanical processes by which they were created.

In the last few decades an important body of scholarship has unpicked the gendered and colonial impulses of Victorian boys' adventure fiction, effec-tively arguing that the genre sought to instil a racially charged nationalism into the empire's future supporters and colonial administrators (see, for instance, Katz; Richards ed.; Bristow; Boyd; Mathison; Kestner; Brantlinger; Deane; and Ehland and Gohrisch eds.). However, this youth-inculcation argument is complicated by the uncertainty that continues to surround adventure fiction's audience. When Stevenson began publishing *Treasure Island* in *Young Folks*, the magazine's editor had to defend the novel from children who complained of the new serial not being 'suited to [their] taste'

Stand of the Greys" [the war at the heart of *King Solomon's Mines*] won't be in it' (p. 233).

('Our Letter Box', 12 November 1881; 'Our Letter Box', 19 November 1881). The youngest protagonist in either *King Solomon's Mines* or *The Lost World*, meanwhile, is twenty-three years old, and most of the other characters in these novels are in their thirties, fifties, and even sixties – a curious age-range for novels supposedly aimed at children.[4] In fact, the only entry on any of these novels in the Open University's Reading Experience Database is from the diary of a twenty-five-year-old Welshman who recorded spending a 'lovely day' reading *The Lost World* while in Germany at the beginning of the First World War (Thomas). More than simply a misalignment of intended and actual audiences, then, I would suggest that – despite how we typically remember the genre today – these boys' adventure novels were always aimed in part at adult readers, in a classic example of what Barbara Wall has termed 'dual address', or a less extreme prefiguring of what Michelle Ann Abate describes as 'the growing genre of … children's literature for adults' (p. 3). Indeed, each of these novels was produced by the general fiction departments of two mainstream/adult publishing houses (Cassell & Company and Hodder and Stoughton). Buy *Treasure Island* for the boys in your life, recommended the Guernsey *Star* in 1883, 'and if the boys will none of it, why then let the purchaser redeem his book, read it himself, and be a boy again' ('A Romance of the Buccaneers', p. 4).[5] As I will return to later on, *King Solomon's Mines*

---

[4] Questions emerge as well over the extent to which these novels had a solely male audience. See, for instance, Haggard's description in his memoirs of how, soon after his violent homosocial novel was first published, 'a girls' school, or some members of it, evidently weary of the society of their own sex, wrote congratulating me with great earnestness because I had in "King Solomon's Mines" produced a thrilling book "without a heroine"' (p. 234). Of course, the somewhat patronising phrase 'with great earnestness' imbues this description with a distancing irony that works to implicitly reinforce the novel's status as a novel meant for only boys and men. Though I have yet to uncover any non-white readers myself, it would be intriguing to explore whether these novels had a racially diverse audience and, if they did, what those readers made of the genre.

[5] See, also, Stevenson's subsequent account of writing *Treasure Island*, in his 1894 essay 'My First Book': 'I had counted on one boy [i.e. Lloyd Osbourne]; I found I had two in my audience. My father caught fire at once with all the romance and childishness of his original nature' (p. 7).

was explicitly dedicated to 'all the big and little boys who read it', and *The Lost World* to 'the boy who's half a man, Or the man who's half a boy'. As a result, I would suggest, the impulse of this often somewhat melancholy genre is less didactic propaganda than personal, civilisational, and material nostalgia (albeit a nostalgia informed by the era's imperialist ideologies).

In 1982, Marshall Berman famously reflected that

> To be modern is to be part of a universe in which, as Marx said, 'all that is solid melts into air'. People who find themselves in the midst of this maelstrom are apt to feel that they are the first ones, and maybe the only ones, to be going through it; [a] feeling that has engendered numerous nostalgic myths of pre-modern Paradise Lost. (pp. 15–16)

The final section of this Element identifies a New Romance revival movement that emerged in the early twenty-first century, in lost world adventure fiction aimed more narrowly at children by Cressida Cowell, Tony DiTerlizzi, and Tom Taylor. Between about 2003 and 2015, it really did feel as if all that was solid might quite literally melt into air, at least when it came to books. As Berman notes here, modernity tends towards ahistorical exceptionalism, and post-millennial anxieties about books losing their physicality to become simply undifferentiated atoms distributed across an amorphous digital 'cloud' typically erase all precedents. Yet, I will argue, the twenty-first-century revival of New Romance – what I am calling New Romance 2.0 – was highly aware of both its 'Golden Age' Victorian pre-history and the dynamics of prelapsarian nostalgia that it simultaneously perpetuated, critiqued, and subverted.

1 Spick and Span New Paper

The book's nineteenth-century dehumanisation centred partly on changes in how paper was made and what it was made from. Since the fifteenth century, practically all of the paper used in Britain had been made from rags: from the linen and cotton undergarments people across Britain and the Continent had worn, on an everyday basis, in the closest possible proximity to their bodies. For four centuries, then, the 'intriguing . . . contacts' that rag paper imaginatively enabled engendered a peculiar sense of transnational intimacy (Senchyne, p. 5). A typical expression of the imaginative world that developed around rag paper can be found, at the very end of the rag-paper era, in Charles Dickens and Mark Lemon's description of visiting a paper mill, in a piece first published in *Household Words* in 1850:

> White, pure, spick and span new paper . . . can it ever come from rags like these? Is it from such bales of dusty rags, native and foreign, of every colour and of every kind, as now environ us, shutting out the summer air and putting cotton into our summer ears, that virgin paper, to be written on, and printed on, proceeds? . . . The coarse blouse of the Flemish labourer, and the fine cambric of the Prussian lady, the court dress of the Austrian jailer, and the miserable garb of the Italian peasant; the woollen petticoat of the Bavarian girl, the linen head-dress of the Neapolitan woman, the priest's vestments, the player's robe, the Cardinal's hat, and the plough-man's nightcap; all dwindle down to this, and bring their littleness or greatness in fractional portions here . . . My conductor leads the way into another room. I am to go, as the rags go, regularly and systematically through the Mill. I am to suppose myself a bale of rags. I *am* rags. (pp. 529–30)

Deborah Wynne has recently emphasised the ways in which Dickens presented paper as a symbol of destitute 'ragged children' and their potential for up-cycling social improvement: 'like rags', Wynne notes, 'cast-off children were', for Dickens, 'capable of being purified and made socially useful' (p. 35). Here, though, rather than perpetuating society's hierarchies, Dickens and Lemon present the rag-based papermaking process as radically equalising. Indeed, this is a process that boils down not just clothing but artificial social distinctions of age, gender, nationality, and class, until rags (and the paper made from them) become a quintessence of universal humanity.

Yet, in many ways, these lines – written at a time of industrial transition – represent a paean to a dying discourse and cultural valence, for the age of rags was coming to an end. While the number of paper mills in Britain doubled over the course of the eighteenth century, the production methods that these mills employed essentially remained those of the first British paper mills, established in the late fifteenth century (Raven, p. 6). A skilled artisan would create one sheet of paper at a time by carefully allowing a rag slurry to form evenly across the wire mesh contained within a wooden frame. As the slurry dried on this mesh, a corresponding 'laid' pattern of chain and wire lines would form, thereby ensuring each sheet of paper a ghostly remnant of its handmade, human origins – a remnant that hovers behind the printed text of pre-industrial books to this day. At the same time, a watermark would often be imprinted into the paper, serving as a physical symbol of the maker's labour and of the paper's authenticity. At the turn of the nineteenth century, however, a far more efficient steam-powered 'Fourdrinier' machine was invented that used a conveyor belt to produce a continuous roll of paper at a far greater speed (see Fig. 1).

These machines proved so efficient that, only two decades after they were first introduced, they accounted for the majority of paper made in Britain (see the annual production figures provided in Spicer, pp. 258–60). Soon, it became clear that the key remaining impediment to meeting Britain's increasing demand for paper was the country's limited supply of the raw component. After much experimentation, alternatives to rag paper were devised. Indeed, rags went from being more or less the sole component of British paper in 1860 to only accounting for around 10 per cent of paper production by the century's end, having been eclipsed by first esparto grass in the early 1870s and then wood pulp twenty years later.[6]

---

[6] For these figures and an accompanying graph, see Magee, pp. 134–6.

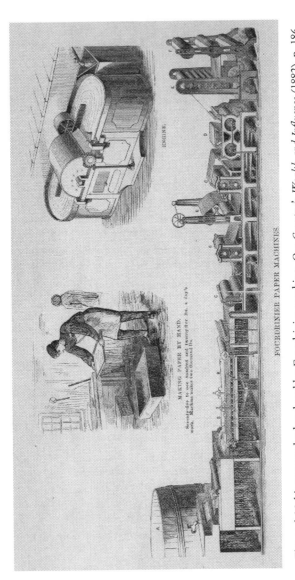

FOURDRINIER PAPER MACHINES

ENGINE.

MAKING PAPER BY HAND.

Figure 1 Making paper by hand and by Fourdrinier machine. *Our Country's Wealth and Influence* (1882), p. 186

– HathiTrust Digital Library

(Etymologically, the 'span' in 'spick and span' relates to woodchips, lending Dickens' description of 'spick and span new paper' a second, proleptic significance. 'Spick and span' was itself originally a shipbuilding phrase meaning 'as new as new nails and woodchips'.)

'One of the first and only significant additions to the Fourdriniers' original machine design', Starre has noted, was the 'dandy roll' – a device that could 'artificially recreate the laid pattern and the watermarks' of handmade paper (p. 131). In other words, much like early printed typefaces imitating handwriting and e-books digitally recreating the physical properties of analogue books today, the initial impulse of industrial bookmaking was over-engineered material nostalgia (see Fig. 2).

Paper made with a dandy roll became a surprisingly contentious cultural material in the late nineteenth century. William Morris, tellingly, took particular exception to the mode of 'sham-fine' mock-authenticity that, he claimed, the dandy roll epitomised. 'If machine-made paper must be used', Morris opined, in an 1893 speech before the Bibliographical Society, 'it should . . . show itself for what it is', instead of 'imitat[ing] the structure of handmade paper' (p. 185).[7] A few years earlier, the union of vatmen had declared that if people wanted 'the genuine article they will, notwithstanding the cost, go in for handmade paper' (quoted in Webb and Webb, p. 422). Yet, as Blackburn wryly noted at the time, 'paper, purporting to be carefully "hand-made" . . . can be bought by the pound in Drury Lane' (Blackburn, p. 206), a notably mixed area of late Victorian London associated with both poverty and illusion.[8] When Hodder and Stoughton printed a 1,000-copy 'presentation edition' of *The Lost World* they did so on noticeably thickset

[7] For more on Morris' aversion to the ways in which commercial print culture 'immerses one in a false reality', see Miller, p. 80.

[8] See, for instance, Frances Hodgson Burnett's 1892 article in *Scribner's Magazine*, 'The Drury Lane Boys' Club', in which she describes the Drury Lane Theatre as a 'fairyland' – a 'kaleidoscopic dream of brilliant light and changing color, of glittering rainbow, troops of fairies with wings, and [costumes] which make them floating flowers, or bees, or birds, or snowflakes' – surrounded by the 'ogres of Hard Life, of Poverty, of Misfortune of Lack of Opportunity, of Ignorance, often of Hopelessness, and Hunger, and Disease' (pp. 676–7).

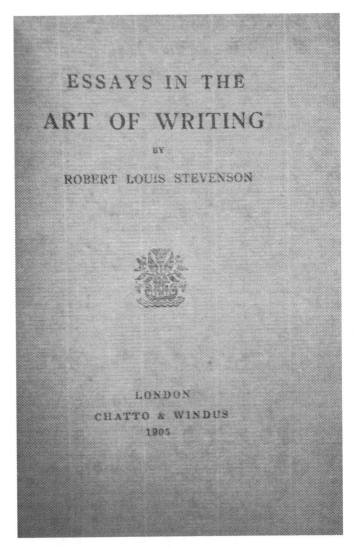

Figure 2 Mock handmade paper, backlit to show the imitation chain and
wire lines. Robert Louis Stevenson, *Essays in the Art of Writing* (1905), title
page – author's personal collection

paper with a rough (or 'deckled') edge. For the most part, though, New Romance novels were subtler in how they recreated the sensation of reading on paper made by hand.

Richard Menke has recently suggested that George Gissing's 1891 work *New Grub Street* 'is the great novel of the transition from rag to esparto to wood-pulp paper because it takes this change as a cue for systematically representing an industrialized culture of print' (p. 78). I suggest that the era's lost world adventure novels constitute even richer examples of the transition from rag to esparto to wood-pulp paper. For, rather than simply 'representing' these changes in a formal or linguistic manner, New Romance novels artificially recreate the materiality of pre-industrial paper in a number of fascinating, complex ways.

I Have a Chart Here

Take, for instance, the maps that lie at the heart of *Treasure Island*, *King Solomon's Mines*, and *The Lost World*. Before they begin exploring Treasure Island, Captain Smollett asks Silver to talk him through the lay of the land:

> 'I have a chart here', says Captain Smollett. 'See if that's the place.' Long John's eyes burned in his head as he took the chart; but, by the fresh look of the paper, I knew he was doomed to disappointment. This was not the map we found in Billy Bones's chest, but an accurate copy, complete in all things – names and heights and soundings – with the single exception of the red crosses and the written notes. (p. 95)

Recent studies of the 'facsimile' maps used in lost world adventure novels tend to describe these maps as teasing or retentive. Indeed, the reader is never given the exact location of Treasure Island, and the map that serves as the frontispiece to Stevenson's novel (see Fig. 3) is underwritten by Jim Hawkins' descriptive note 'Facsimile of chart; latitude and longitude struck out' (p. [i]). 'Like Jim's pirates', Jean Fernandez argues, 'the frustrated reader must therefore contend with an inaccurate copy' of an absent original (p. 45), while Sally Bushell has similarly emphasised the ways in which

Figure 3 Robert Louis Stevenson, *Treasure Island* (Cassell & Company, 1897), frontispiece map and title page –

Stevenson's frontispiece 'silently withholds vital information' (i.e. the directions to the buried treasure chest supposedly written on the back of the map) (p. 625). What this somewhat prosecutorial perspective elides, however, is that fictional eighteenth-century pirates and historical nineteenth-century novel readers interacted with Stevenson's map in different ways. Indeed, whereas Stevenson's characters usually employ a highly instrumentalist approach to cartographic descriptions of Treasure Island, for Stevenson's readers this map is the key not to gold bullion but to imaginative pleasure. And, rather than expressing 'frustration' or 'disappointment' with what the frontispiece map does not include, Stevenson's early reviewers instead wrote of the map being 'delightful', 'got up in strict eighteenth-century guise', and 'adding to the De Foe air of realism' (Henley; 'A Romance of the Buccaneers'; 'The Literary Field'). What these readers praise, then, is the map's playfully antiquated theatricality.

Before even leaving for Treasure Island, Hawkins 'brood[s] by the hour over the map' that he has found, using it to 'approach that island in my fancy' (p. 54). Unlike the map Smollett shows Silver in the above passage, the map Stevenson shows his readers does, pointedly, contain a remarkably convincing reproduction of the original's highly evocative 'red crosses and written notes', and I would argue that Stevenson's frontispiece map enables a kind of meta or second-order imagination. While Hawkins' map helps him to imagine Treasure Island, the reader's map helps them to imagine the materiality of Hawkins' map, the worn, yellowed (p. 243) paper on which it is drawn, and the world of pre-industrial print culture that it metonymically represents. In this, *Treasure Island* effectively reconfigures and repurposes what was, by Stevenson's period, already coming to be seen as the central deficiency of modern esparto and wood-pulp paper: its tendency to age and discolour far more quickly than its pre-industrial rag counterpart (for nineteenth-century discussions of this problem, see 'Effect of the Electric Light upon Books'; 'Why Does Paper Turn Yellow?'; 'The Selection of Paper'; 'Notices of Books: The Art of Paper-Making'). In the case of *Treasure Island*, then, what would otherwise simply be a deficiency instead works to ensure Stevenson's frontispiece map – and early editions of his novel more broadly – an ever-greater lacquer of material verisimilitude over time, as the reader's map increasingly comes to resemble that used by

Jim, rather than Silver's copy of the map drawn on disappointingly 'fresh'-looking paper. Indeed, this is especially true as, over the years, the tissue paper ostensibly designed to protect this frontispiece in some early editions of Stevenson's novel actually stains the map with a faint mustardy tinge (see Fig. 3). As Jean Baudrillard notes of Borges' full-scale map in 'Of Exactitude in Science', 'the double ends by being confused with the real through aging' (p. 1).

The same is true of the facsimile frontispiece map tipped in to early editions of *King Solomon's Mines* (see Fig. 4). Wendy Katz has written of Haggard's 'personal sense of frustration with his society's growing attachment to machines, industry, and urban living' (p. 30), and the original, diegetic map that Haggard's facsimile invokes is even more explicit in its pre-industrial material anachronism than Stevenson's map in *Treasure Island*. In fact, we are told that this original map was drawn not simply on rag paper but on an actual rag – on a fragment of material ('upon a remnant of my raiment'; p. 28) torn from the shirt of a minor character's sixteenth-century ancestor, José da Silvestra. Here, then, the industrial esparto paper on which the reader's facsimile is actually printed becomes a kind of atavistic medium for its own pre-industrial material ancestor, superimposing the somatic intimacy implicit within rag paper onto this modern page. In a strange way, the civilisational nostalgia of facsimile rag paper would have arguably been reinforced by a personal nostalgia for many of Haggard's early readers, as, in this period, 'indestructible' linen was typically used instead of paper in illustrated 'toy books' aimed at very young children (see the advertisements 'Aunt Louisa's Toy Books' and 'Catalogue of Toy Books').

Haggard especially commissioned his sister-in-law to produce an actual cloth fragment for this facsimile to be based upon (How, p. 14), and the self-conscious materiality of Haggard's frontispiece is further heightened by its detailed reproduction of a series of material imperfections, such as creases, ink stains, patches of grime, and the tattered, strikingly haphazard, and in several places torn outer fringe of the original rag.

In this, just as the *Treasure Island* frontispiece contained within it the seeds of its future perfecting decay, so too the frontispiece in *King Solomon's Mines*.

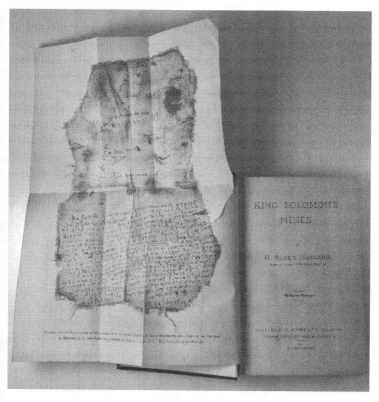

Figure 4 H. Rider Haggard, *King Solomon's Mines* (Cassell & Company, 1886), fold-out frontispiece map and title page – author's personal collection

Far larger than the facsimile map in *Treasure Island*, Haggard's facsimile expands out to become several times the size of his otherwise duodecimo novel. However, the physical mechanics of folding out Haggard's map are surprisingly complex, leading to another strange double *trompe-l'œil* effect. For, today, the paper on which this map is printed routinely features not only real fold lines (in an echo of the mock fold lines depicted in the image) but also a commonly found meta layer of actual tears created, in the last 135 years, by Haggard's insufficiently dexterous readers.

Indeed, Haggard seems to have delighted in the confounding uncategorisability of his frontispiece facsimile and in the uncertainty surrounding its relationship with both its diegetic and physical originals. In first an interview with Harry How in the *Strand* (one of a series of celebrity interviews in that magazine) and then his own autobiography, Haggard recounted how – while travelling on the London Underground to have his original commissioned map and manuscript bound together – he observed an elderly lady opposite him closely studying the map in a printed copy of *King Solomon's Mines*. Yielding to temptation, Haggard brought out and began conspicuously studying his commissioned map, before catching the eye of his fellow passenger, who 'stared first at her map and then at mine, and stared and stared . . . Suddenly, as we were about to leave a station, she sprang up and leapt from the train, at which, the unfolded map still in her hand, she gazed bewildered until it vanished into the tunnel' (Haggard, 'Days of My Life', pp. 234–5; see also How, p. 14). In both Haggard's book itself and the epitextual framework that Haggard constructed around his novel, then, one finds the same play of fake-original and fake-copy, of age (Haggard's fellow passenger is repeatedly referred to as an 'old lady') and modernity (though opened in 1868, London's first Underground line was only completed in 1884).

Drawn on the Bark of a Tree

At first glance, Doyle's map in *The Lost World* bears no connection to those in *Treasure Island* and *King Solomon's Mines* (see Fig. 5). Instead of double frames and verisimilitudinous visual complexity, Doyle's map – a naive horizontal frieze of eighteen irregular lines representing paths through a system of caves – is marked by minimalism and a stark visual simplicity; rather than being a bold opening frontispiece, Doyle's map quietly occupies only a small fraction of a page hidden away in the novel's penultimate chapter. Indeed, at first, Doyle's characters (and, presumably, many of his readers) do not even realise that Doyle's map is a map.

Yet, in many ways, this image can also be seen as a latter-day reflection on (and inflection of) the materially focused pre-modernising work being

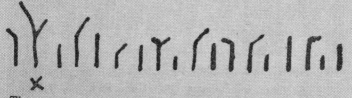

I took the slip of bark to the firelight and we examined it together. It was about a foot square, and on the inner side there was a singular arrangement of lines, which I here reproduce :

They were neatly done in charcoal upon the white surface, and looked to me at first sight like some sort of rough musical score.

Figure 5 Arthur Conan Doyle, *The Lost World* (Hodder and Stoughton, 1912), p. 287 – author's personal collection

performed by the earlier New Romance maps discussed above. When it first appeared in the *Strand*'s serialisation of *The Lost World*, Doyle's map simply echoed the visual language of maps in *Treasure Island* and *King Solomon's Mines*: fictional tears emphasised the frayed, uneven fringe of the material on which the eighteen lines were supposedly drawn, while the coarse texture of this material was further highlighted by worn markings rendered in fine granular detail (see Fig. 6).[9]

However, the nature of this underlying material made for one key point of difference. For, rather than a fragment of rag or a sheet of rag paper, this map was supposedly inscribed, by an Indigenous chieftain, on 'a small roll of the bark of a tree' (p. 287). By doing away with the *Strand*'s simulacra frames to reproduce only the eighteen charcoal lines themselves, early book

---

[9] For a discussion of the *Strand*'s use of 'diegetic illustrations' in Doyle's Sherlock Holmes stories, see Vranken (pp. 68–72).

THE INDIAN CHART OF THE CAVES, DRAWN ON THE BARK OF A TREE.

Figure 6 Arthur Conan Doyle, 'The Lost World: Chapter XV (continued)',
The Strand Magazine (November 1912), p. 483 – McPherson Library,
University of Victoria

editions of *The Lost World* also do away with the map's 'facsimile' status,
further blurring the boundary between the chieftain's technologically
ancient piece of bark and the reader's sheet of early twentieth-century
industrial timber paper (as mentioned above, wood pulp had been the
primary component of paper in Britain since the early 1890s). As readers,
then, it is as if the Indigenous chieftain has drawn directly onto our sheet of
paper, returning books to their etymological origins ('book', from '*Buch*',
beech tree),[10] and re-inscribing in the process a sense of reassuring intimacy
and tradition onto what was otherwise a potentially alienating modern
material and medium. Indeed, only a few pages earlier, the reader is told

---

[10] It is typically claimed that the word 'book' derives from the Old German word
for 'beech tree', certain Germanic tribes having written on both the bark of trees
and wooden writing tablets (Durkin).

that, amongst the tribe to whom the chieftain belongs, tree bark is also worn as clothing (p. 281).[11]

The frontispiece maps in *Treasure Island* and *King Solomon's Mines* are how those fictional adventures begin – within the novels, they act as guides enabling characters to set out in search of the pre-modern worlds they seek. Early in *The Lost World*, on the other hand, Professor Challenger provides his exploration party with a sheet of (presumably industrial) paper that turns out to be blank. They will not need a map to find where they are going, he explains; he has been there before (pp. 104–6). An awareness of itself as a late addition to the New Romance genre pervades Doyle's novel, written as it was twenty-five years after Stevenson's and Haggard's (the very title of Doyle's novel hints at generic self-reflection), and, instead of directing attention towards the ancient and exotic, Doyle's bark map, encountered at the end of *The Lost World*, tells his characters how to begin their journey back to the modern world. It is as if New Romance has finally got over the loss of rag paper as a discursive nexus and is ready to re-historicise wood pulp on its own terms – not by superimposing rag paper onto wood-pulp paper à la *Treasure Island* and *King Solomon's Mines* but by rediscovering the longue-durée history of wood as itself an intimate human technology.[12]

---

[11] It is worth noting that another map appears slightly earlier in *The Lost World*. This 'Rough Chart' of the prehistoric plateau shares the naive, diegetic characteristics of the cave-system map discussed above. The publishing history of the Rough Chart also echoes the cave-system map's movement away from facsimile framing: when the Rough Chart appeared in the *Strand*, it was separated from Doyle's text by a visual border – a border not subsequently included in the first edition of Doyle's book.

[12] See, for instance, Edward Pinto's history of treen – that 'miscellanea of small wooden objects in daily domestic or farm use' that had formed part of everyday life in Britain since at least the Roman occupation (p. 2).

2 Written As Well As Printed by a Steam Engine

Of course, shifts in paper production represent only one part of a far larger set of innovations that collectively transformed how books were made in the Victorian era, and the material experimentation of lost world adventure novels was also deeply informed by a desire to symbolically counteract or discursively re-signify the nineteenth-century automation of printing and literary production more broadly.

From the moment William Caxton imported Gutenberg's technology, in the late fifteenth century, British printing had always involved a great deal of human labour. Individual pieces of type would be cast by hand, before later being painstakingly arranged in what was called a printing 'form'; the type secured in place by this form would then have to be pummelled with inked leather balls; the sheet of paper being used would have to be carefully dampened so as to be able to receive the ink; a human being would then strain on a lever, lowering a platen and squeezing the inked type onto the paper, which would then have to be hung up to dry and folded a number of times until it was the size of the book's desired format; finally, these individual pages would then have to be bound and their edges cut, again by hand. Over the course of the nineteenth century, however, each of these manual processes was automated. For much of technophilic middle-class Britain, these developments spoke simply of progress – this was nothing but a discarding of processes that were 'not only very labourious but very slow'. 'In every element', declared the industrial journalist John Southward, in 1897, 'the book of to-day is as superior to that of 1837 as the locomotive of to-day is to that of the time of Robert Stephenson' (pp. 31, 22).[13] At the same time, however, an anxious counter-discourse emerged that asked what effect this removal of the human might have on the status and significance of books as objects and whether these substructural changes might somehow bleed up to automate and cheapen writing as well.

---

[13] A modern facsimile of Southward's book – Progress in Printing and the Graphic Arts during the Victorian Era – can be found in the Cambridge Library Collection's nineteenth-century reprint series History of Printing, Publishing and Libraries.

A System of Machinery

Publishing histories typically single out 1814 as a milestone in the industrialisation of printing: this was the year *The Times* became the first major document printed on a steam press. And, indeed, in an editorial statement announcing the change, the paper's editor, John Walter, lauded Friedrich Koenig's invention as 'the greatest improvement connected with printing since the discovery of the art itself':

> A system of machinery almost organic has been devised and arranged, which, while it relieves the human frame of its most laborious efforts in printing, far exceeds all human powers in rapidity and dispatch ... After the letters are placed by the compositors in what is called the form, little more remains for man to do, than to attend upon, and watch this unconscious agent in its operations. The machine is then merely supplied with paper: itself places the form, inks it, adjusts the paper to the form newly inked, stamps the sheet, and gives it forth to the hands of the attendant. ([Walter])

In this statement, the line between mechanical and human printer is radically and explicitly blurred. Whereas Koenig's invention represents an 'almost organic ... unconscious agent', the human printers it replaces were themselves only ever 'human frames'. The humans who are still required persist as little more than the machine's 'attendants', subordinate fleshy prostheses within a mixed cyborgian system. Indeed, the adolescents who performed this role actually came to be known as 'machine boys',[14] in a prefiguring of Marx's claim that industrial working conditions were 'transforming the workman, from his very childhood, into a part of a detail-machine' (pp. 421–2).

Clearly, *The Times*' ontological ambiguity is principally designed to ease the transition away from human labour at a time of Luddite rebellion.[15]

---

[14] See H. W. Lord's report on child labour within the printing industry for Britain's 1865 Royal Commission, p. 2.

[15] Walter famously installed Koenig's machines under the cover of darkness before dismissing his human printers the next morning, at which stage, Walter's 1847

For equating human and mechanical labour is part of reducing each down to matters of comparative efficiency – to rationalising arguments of 'rapidity and dispatch'. Yet this approach also left the publication open to humanist critique, and, eighteen months later, William Hazlitt derisively defined *The Times* as 'that prodigious prosing paper ... which seems to be written as well as printed by a steam-engine' ('Theatrical Examiner', p. 379). 'It is elaborate, but heavy', Hazlitt went on to declare, in 1823, 'full, but not readable: it is stuffed up with official documents, with matter-of-fact details. It seems intended to be deposited in the office of the Keeper of the Records, and might be imagined to be composed as well as printed with a steam-engine' ('Periodical Press', p. 363). For several decades, the cost of steam-powered machines meant the use of this new technology was largely confined to newspaper printing (Feather, p. 89). However, as the machines became increasingly ubiquitous in Britain so too did the kind of conceptual slippage that Hazlitt here employs, confounding industrial printing and industrial writing. Moreover, just as in Hazlitt, this rhetorical manoeuvre typically tapped in to a broader critical perception of the nineteenth century as an age of literary overproduction: an age, to quote Karin Littau, of 'too much print, too much writing, too much reading' (p. 4).

Thus, in 1825, Sir Walter Scott's *Tales of the Crusaders* – a compendium of the twentieth and twenty-first contributions to the Waverley series – begins with a character self-parodically suggesting that 'some part of the labour of composition of these novels might be saved by the use of steam', at least when it comes to their narratological 'common-places' (pp. xiii–xix). Twenty years later, *Punch* went further still, publishing a facetious set of mock testimonials averring the efficacy of 'Mr. Babbage's Patent Novel-Writer'. 'By its assistance', attested a satiric fictionalisation of G. P. R. James, the startlingly prolific mid-Victorian romance writer,

> I am now enabled to complete a novel in 3 vols. 8vo., of the usual size, in the short space of 48 hours; whereas before, at least a fortnight's labour was requisite for that purpose ...

obituary in *The Times* recalls, he warned his printers that 'if they attempted violence there was a force ready to suppress it' ('Death of Mr. Walter').

Some days [ago] I placed my hero and heroine, peasants of
Normandy, in the surprising-adventure-department of the
engine; set the machinery in motion, and, on letting off the
steam a few hours after, found the one a Duke, and the other
a Sovereign Princess; they having become so by the most
natural and interesting process in the world.

('The New Patent Novel Writer')

Sandwiched within this mock testimonial, *Punch* featured an illustrative
cartoon explicitly tying this critical conceit back not just to Charles
Babbage's early computers but to the era's changes in printing technology
(see Fig. 7).

In 1814, Walter described how *The Times'* new cylindrical machine
required only to be supplied with paper before it would 'itself place the
form, ink it, stamp the sheet, and give it forth to the hands of the
attendant'. In *Punch*'s cartoon, a Jamesian figure wearing a printer's
hat (in this vision, author and printer are indistinguishable) feeds a long
scroll of paper featuring his French peasants into a cylindrical steam-
powered machine of his own. On the other side of the machine,
a diminutive 'machine boy' receives the paper, peasants magically
transformed into aristocrats, à la industrial capitalism's broader promise
of socio-economic transformation.[16] In the background, James' earlier
novels, among them *The False Heir* (1843) and *Agincourt* (1844), hang up
to dry.

In 1865, H. W. Lord reported that, in Britain, 'the bulk of printed
matter . . . is produced by the agency of steam-power' (p. 3), while, twenty
years later, Frederick Wilson declared that 'nearly every printing-office' in
the country 'now possesses [an] automatic or self-acting . . . machine'
(pp. 1–2). Clearly, then, by the time of the late Victorian adventure
novel, automatic printing had become the norm. Indeed, in Cassell &
Company, *Treasure Island* and *King Solomon's Mines* reached the public

---

[16] With thanks to Clara Tuite for pointing out this broader socio-economic
resonance.

Figure 7 'The New Patent Novel Writer', *Punch, or the London Charivari*
(14 December 1844), p. 268 – Universitätsbibliothek Heidelberg

through a publishing firm 'proud of [its] machinery … then considered to
be the very acme of progress' (*The Story of the House of Cassell*, p. 220). By
1861, Cassell's 'Belle Sauvage' printing works was even selling a 'hand-
press superseding' steam press of their own (see Fig. 8).

At the same time, though, each of these New Romance novels works to
radically reconfigure the kind of cultural valences afforded to them as
industrial literary products by the discourse traced above.

THE HAND-PRESS SUPERSEDED BY   THE PATENT "BELLE SAUVAGE" MACHINE

PETTER AND GALPIN'S PATENT "BELLE SAUVAGE" PRINTING MACHINE,

LONDON, E.C.

The Cheapest and most Valuable Single Cylinder Machine for general purposes ever produced.

THE PATENT

"BELLE SAUVAGE" PRINTING MACHINE

Is constructed on principles combining simplicity and durability with speed and economy, and is acknowledged to be unquestionably the most perfect and useful Machine ever yet introduced for Newspaper, Book, and First-class Jobbing Works, Broadsides, &c. &c.

The MACHINE occupies *but little space*, is *sufficiently light* to admit of its being erected in an ordinary Press-room, and can be *driven with ease by Hand*, or by Steam Power, at the rate of 1,000 impressions per hour.

☞ The Machine may be viewed in Operation, original Testimonials seen, and further information obtained, upon application to Messrs. PETTER and GALPIN, Patentees and Manufacturers, Belle Sauvage Works, Ludgate Hill, London, E.C.

Figure 8 The 'Belle Sauvage' Steam-Powered Printing Machine (advertisement), *Cassell's Illustrated History of England: Volume V* (1861), p. 156[b] – The British Library

A Last Tattered Notebook

In many ways, Stevenson, Haggard, and Doyle were themselves quasi-industrial professionals who shared G. P. R. James' uncanny ability to churn out novels with great regularity and speed: 'A chapter a day I mean to do', Stevenson told his fellow writer W. E. Henley while writing *Treasure Island*.[17] Internally, however, their novels typically present the process by which they were created as something far more organic and romantically primordial. Thus, whereas one of the principal critiques of industrially printed material was its excessive length – what Hazlitt called its 'prodigious prosing' – adventure fiction pre-empted by a decade the more widespread shortening of British novels in the mid-1890s. As children's novels written in large part for adults, *Treasure Island*, *King Solomon's Mines*, and *The Lost World* were published as single volumes and were therefore considerably shorter than the adult market's traditional triple-deckers. Indeed, whereas these New Romance texts ranged from 70,000 to 85,000 words, each of Scott's novels in *Tales of the Crusaders*, for instance, contained around 135,000 words, James' *Agincourt* 180,000, and Gissing's *New Grub Street* a full 200,000.

When, in 1894, the compact between Mudie's Select Library and the large British publishers fell apart, *The Times* refused to believe that anything would change, declaring 'whatever the future has in store, it will never bring publishers to issue in one volume a . . . novel which fits naturally into three' ('London, Wednesday', p. 10.) Immediately, Haggard wrote to the newspaper to object, publicly (and, as it would turn out, correctly) predicting that the death of Mudie's compact with British publishers would in turn mean the death of three-volume publication – a death which would be mourned, he claimed, by no one other than 'paper-makers, printers, and binders' ('The Three-Volume Novel').

---

[17] 'It's awful fun boys' stories', Stevenson continues, 'no trouble, no strain . . . no writing, just drive along as the words come and the pen will scratch!' ('To W. E. Henley', p. 259). In his memoirs, Haggard claimed to have written *King Solomon's Mines* in 'about six weeks' (1926, p. 226), though scholars have subsequently corrected this to thirteen, based on a reading of Haggard's notebooks from the period (Hampson, p. 44). Doyle appears to have written *The Lost World* in around ten weeks (see Carr, p. 258).

Ten years earlier, anticipating this authorial attitude, Haggard's narrator begins *King Solomon's Mines* by making explicit the novel's drive for descriptive selectivity, announcing that the work which follows

> does not pretend to be a full account of everything we did and saw. There are many things connected with our journey into Kukuanaland that I should have liked to dwell upon at length, and which have, as it is, been scarcely alluded to . . . I thought . . . that the best plan would be to tell the story in a plain, straightforward manner [without] the grand literary flights and flourishes which I see in novels. (pp. v–vi)

Here, then, Haggard employs the gruffly masculine (and conspicuously 'authentic') voice of boys' adventure fiction to create a moment of playful self-reflexivity, establishing a form of literary self-consciousness that will pervade both his fictional non-fiction novel and the New Romance movement more generally. In so doing, the movement actively pre-empts and resists charges of mindless industrial overproduction and generic automatism.

In 1887, Haggard declared 'the love of romance . . . coeval with the existence of humanity', 'flourish[ing] as strongly in the barbarian as in the cultured breast' ('About Fiction', p. 172), and, in attempting to repel accusations of mindless industrial modernity, the lost world novels of New Romance typically associate their own production with explicitly pre-modern modes of storytelling. In the process, these novels superimpose a complex, ambivalent (and, at times, even contradictory) set of values onto late Victorian projections of pre-modern or Indigenous practices and culture. Indeed, as Bradley Deane has noted, lost world novels such as these reflect 'the apparent paradox of an imperialism that openly embraces the primitive' (p. 147). Thus, whereas *The Lost World* is narrated by a member of that most Victorian of professions, journalism, Malone makes a particular point of emphasising the primitive conditions under which he has written much of his account, supposedly completed on a meat-tin with 'a worn stub of pencil and a last, tattered note-book' (p. 276). In an even more overt fashion, Haggard's narrator explains his literary approach by way of a traditional (fictional) tribal aphorism: '"A sharp spear", runs the Kukuana saying, "needs no polish"; and on the same principle I venture to hope that a true story, however strange it may be, does not require to be decked out in fine words' (p. vi).

Yet, New Romance also confounds Victorian critiques of the supposed anonymity or mechanicity of industrial printing by re-imbuing the medium in which modern literature appeared with a distinctive essentialist psychology. One of the great innovations of this second printing revolution was chromolithography and the cheap, widely available colour illustrations that it enabled (Feather, p. 90). Indeed, in 1880, the first director of the South Kensington Museum, Sir Henry Cole, noted that reductions in production costs meant that children's books illustrated with chromolithographs were now being sold at one-tenth of the price of the hand-coloured illustrations that he had commissioned for his nursery rhyme books only forty years earlier (quoted in Whalley, pp. 20–1). Stevenson's frontispiece map (see Fig. 3) fully exploits these economic and technological transformations.[18] For the palimpsestic effect on which this map relies itself depends on the popular printer's – still relatively new-found – ability to produce large commercial print runs in multiplied-coloured inks: Captain Flint's annotations are written in red, Billy Bones' in brown, and Jim Hawkins' in blue. Two years later, Haggard similarly relied on the use of red ink in particular for maintaining the illusion that his frontispiece had been drawn in da Silvestra's blood (see Fig. 4). In both instances, then, cheap modern printing imbues these maps with not just verisimilitude but characterological individuation, becoming a materialisation of these characters' distinctive inner beings (and, in da Silvestra's case, literally the ink that runs through their veins). Rather than cold anonymity, these maps proclaim industrial printing's potential for intimate, organic personalisation.

[18] In 1887, Henry Wood recorded 'the printing of maps' to be 'one of the most frequent applications of chromolithography to book illustration' (p. 11).

3 Tottery Characters

While the use of colour adds to the power of these cartographic annotations, their status as facsimiles of handwriting ensured that (even if they had not been coloured) these notes would have held a particular significance for readers in the late nineteenth and early twentieth centuries. 'Have you ever had occasion to study character in handwriting?', Holmes asks Watson in Doyle's 1890 novel *The Sign of the Four:*

> 'What do you make of this fellow's scribble?' 'It is legible and regular', I answered. 'A man of business habits and some force of character.' Holmes shook his head. 'Look at the long letters', he said. 'They hardly rise above the common herd. That *d* might be an *a*, and that *l* an *e*. Men of character always differentiate their long letters, however illegibly they may write.' (p. 155)

Just before this moment in their dialogue, Watson accuses Holmes of being 'an automaton – a calculating machine', telling him, 'There is something positively inhuman in you at times' (p. 155). Graphology's popularity at the end of the nineteenth century is typically tied to a far larger wave of pseudoscientific body-reading enthusiasms (encompassing everything from phrenology to physiognomy to cheiromancy) that washed over *fin-de-siècle* Europe (see, for instance, Rains). While acknowledging graphology's symbiotic relationship with a broader discursive network of popular scientific practices and beliefs, I suggest the renewed attention that handwriting received in this period was also more specifically a reaction against that other great technology mechanising the sphere of literary production – the typewriter. Typically of the New Romance movement, however, these authors were only able to include so many material markers of anti-mechanical resistance in their novels because they had access to new industrial processes that made the mass printing of handwriting facsimiles economically and technologically viable in the first place – an ideological complexity I will explore in greater detail at the end of this section.

Extinction Rebellion

In Sections 1 and 2, we saw how new printing and papermaking technologies were viewed as devices that might replace older handicrafts in ways that threatened to automate and dehumanise literary production. The same discourse developed around the typewriter. 'The Sholes and Gliddens Type Writer', declared advertisements in 1876, 'supersedes the pen for all kinds of manuscript writing' ('The Type Writer' (advertisement)). 'If the use of this machine becomes general', the *Flintshire Herald* fretted, 'handwriting will become as completely superseded as handsewing' ('Writing Superseded'). *The Times*, conversely, celebrated this apparent technological progress, declaring that 'the art of writing is now threatened with extinction', typewritten script 'superseding handwriting by a mechanical process' ('The Type Writer'). Here, in this language of 'extinction', handwriting becomes a corporealised species, a kind of dinosaur, rhetorically transformed into a creature of flesh and blood in a conceptual echo of the shift from corporeal rag paper to machine paper outlined in Section 1.

In her history of handwriting in America, Tamara Thornton has argued that the invention of the typewriter changed the cultural valence of handwriting in two key ways. The first was to imbue all forms of handwriting with a level of nostalgia going forward. In a moment that unwittingly both demonstrates the logic of nostalgia and underlines the lasting power of this specific metaphor, Thornton serendipitously revisits the language of 'extinction' used by *The Times* more than 120 years earlier:

> the major consequence of the typewriter and computer for penmanship was not the extinction of handwriting but its symbolic association with the past. Precisely because it seemed to be outmoded, the skill of penmanship came to symbolise a world fast disappearing or already gone. For those who yearned for times past [handwriting] promised to turn the clock back and stave off the ill effects of modernity. (p. 180)

At the same time, Thornton notes, typewriters also indirectly strengthened those associative bonds linking handwriting to 'the individualized self' (p. 114). For, at the end of the nineteenth century, 'the distinctiveness of handwriting [came] to signify the persistence of individuality in the face of homogenizing pressures' (pp. 113–14). Indeed, while she relies on other evidence in constructing her argument, Thornton's conclusions are further reinforced by the flood of newspaper and magazine advertisements for 'The Calli-Graphic Pen' in the early-to-mid 1880s: 'The Calli-Graphic Pen ... a luxury to persons who care to preserve their individuality in writing' ('The Calli-Graphic Pen'). As if to make clear the new reason for this 'preservation' being necessary, when these advertisements appeared in journals they often appeared on the same page as advertisements for 'The Caligraph' typewriter ('The Ideal Writing Machine: The Caligraph').

Throughout the late nineteenth and early twentieth centuries, then, handwriting was widely held to be psychologically revelatory. 'The dissimulating, the obstinate, the idle man', Rosa Baughan declared in 1880, 'all aptitudes bad or good, all sensations, even those that are the most fugitive, are betrayed to the graphologist in a simple letter' (p. 4). Students of graphology who 'make a minute examination' of a given script, Henry Frith assured his readers in 1886 (quoting an unnamed authority), will be able to 'ascertain, from the traces of the pen on the paper, the movements and tendency of the mind, "and thus find out the prevailing passions and habits as directed by the soul and the brain"' of the writer (p. 20). Even those sceptical of graphologists' bolder claims tended to concede that handwriting maintained some connection with the writer's inner world. 'Handwriting', suggested W. A. Spooner in 1888, 'like almost all unconscious, or semi-conscious action, lets out secrets' (p. 657). (For more on literary representations of graphology in this period, see Koehler.)

It is within this discursive context, I would suggest, that we should view the conspicuousness of handwriting in New Romance texts. In Stevenson's 1886 novel, Jekyll and Hyde are first identified as one person by an amateur graphologist who tellingly notes that their 'two hands are in many points identical: only differently sloped', and that their shared handwriting is that of a man who is if not 'mad', at least 'odd' (pp. 51–2). In *Treasure Island*, we are actually provided with characters' handwriting (see Fig. 4), and even greater emphasis is placed on constructing (and then interpreting the significance of) individual characters' differing scripts. Indeed, Stevenson subsequently claimed that, in creating the map that begins *Treasure Island*, 'my father . . . brought into service a knack he had of various writing, and elaborately *forged* the signature of Captain Flint, and the sailing directions of Billy Bones' (Stevenson's emphasis, p. 10). Here, we again encounter the complex, even contradictory, ontological conceits of New Romance fiction – what Saler terms the movement's 'ironic imagination' (pp. 30–40). For, even while explicitly reminding readers of the 'elaborate' collaborative authorial work that went into constructing his fictional text, in labelling his father's calligraphic ventriloquisms 'forgeries', Stevenson also maintains an illusion of authentic diegetic actuality (Flint's handwriting can only be considered to have been 'forged' if Flint himself really exists). The language of forgery, then, speaks to the central tensions of New Romance, counterpointing and intermixing as the genre does notions of the fake and the original, traditional handicrafts (à la the forge) and modern automation. Indeed, it did so only a few years after the first modern British trademark legislation of 1875 implicitly acknowledged the difficulties of establishing and demonstrating unique authenticity in an age of mass consumerism and mechanical reproduction, defining a registerable mark as either a name, a distinctive symbol, or 'a written signature or copy of a written signature' ('An Act to Establish a Register of Trade Marks', p. 5; see also, Bentley, p. 22).

Yet, within the world of *Treasure Island*, it is clear that we, as readers, are meant to view the handwriting samples that Stevenson provides as characterologically telling. On the frontispiece map, Jim points out, Captain Flint's red-inked annotations are written 'in a small, neat hand, very different from [Billy Bones'] tottery characters' in brown (p. 51) (see Fig. 9).

The supposed insights of graphologists were famously slippery and deliberately difficult to pin down. Here, though, what might be termed the 'bio-hermeneutics' of graphology become fairly straightforward, turning calligraphic characters into metonyms for the literary characters who supposedly produced them. Like his 'small, neat', blood-red handwriting, Flint's menace stems in part from his anally retentive and methodically calculating acts of violence and intimidation – first murdering and then

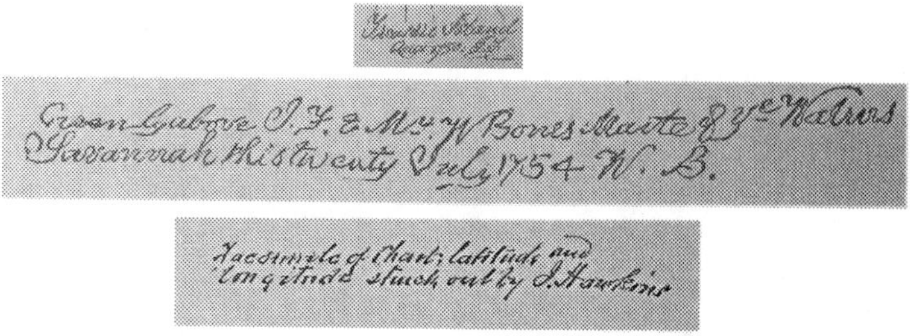

Figure 9 Robert Louis Stevenson, *Treasure Island* (Cassell & Company, 1897), details from frontispiece map – author's personal collection

carefully positioning one of his crew members, for instance, so that his corpse aligned perfectly with the compass and could be used by subsequent treasure hunters to take a bearing (p. 264). When Jim first introduces us to Billy Bones, meanwhile, he describes him as 'a tall, heavy nut-brown man' who used to sing sea shanties in an 'old tottering voice' (pp. 1–2).

Jim makes no reference to his own handwriting on the map; however, the extent to which a reading of Flint's and Bones' handwriting is first invited and then rewarded seems to encourage us to analyse his handwriting as well. Other than the appropriately uncomplicated regularity of Jim's writing, perhaps the most notable aspect of this sample is the way in which the final word, 'Hawkins', falls off at the end. A year before Stevenson wrote *Treasure Island*, in perhaps the best-known graphology manual of the period, Baughan claimed that writing which 'run[s] down at the termination of the lines announces ill health, or profound melancholy, and therefore a troubled and disappointed life' (p. 5); and, in the final sentence of Stevenson's novel, Jim describes how the events of the story continue to haunt him: 'the worst dreams that ever I have are when I hear the surf booming about its coasts, or start upright in bed, with the sharp voice of Captain Flint still ringing in my ears' (p. 292). The very fact that Jim's writing is rendered in blue – a colour consistently associated with pirates in

Stevenson's novel[19] – itself seems suggestive, as if Jim's life and personality have been indelibly stained by the characters with whom he has associated. Again, then, New Romance blurs lines separating bibliographical form from literary content, nostalgically re-imbuing modern books with the corporeal significance of pre-industrial books and manuscripts. Indeed, it seems telling that when arguably the most maligned character in Stevenson's novel – the ironically named and clinically rule-obsessed pirate insurrectionist George Merry – delivers Silver his notice of deposition, Silver responds, 'very pretty wrote, to be sure, like print, I swear' (p. 240), in a moment that seems to implicitly condemn Stevenson's late Victorian print-culture world of antiromantic bureaucracy.

Like *Treasure Island*, the text of *The Lost World* suggests that sympathetic links exist between its characters' handwriting and their respective personalities: that prickly man of steel, Professor Challenger, we are told, has handwriting 'like a barbed-wire railing' (p. 29). Yet perhaps the most notably conspicuous example of handwriting in *The Lost World* (or, indeed, arguably any New Romance novel)[20] takes on a function that is more complex still. It can be found debossed into the front cover of the novel's standard first edition (see Fig. 10).

On this front cover, we find a gold-stamped image of Professor Challenger sitting at a desk, using an inkwell to write on one of three haphazardly strewn sheets of paper. Hovering underneath this image – in

---

[19]   Throughout his time in Jim's inn, Bones wears a 'soiled blue coat' (p. 1); when Bones encounters his fellow-pirate Black Dog, his nose turns blue (p. 13); Flint is said to have worn a blue headscarf (p. 124); when Silver goes to negotiate with Smollett, he goes 'tricked out in his best', namely 'an immense blue coat'; and Flint's face is repeatedly described as having been blue as a result of the over-consumption of rum (p. 268). Of course, the figure of 'Bluebeard' also hovers behind this association.

[20]   Another example of a New Romance novel that contains notably-conspicuous facsimile handwriting is John Uri Lloyd's wonderfully strange book *Etidorhpa, or, the End of Earth* (1896), early editions of which contain manuscript letters (one of these letters is even addressed to the reader). However, as a metaphysical American novel, rather than a British boys' adventure fiction story, Lloyd's work falls outside of this Element's remit.

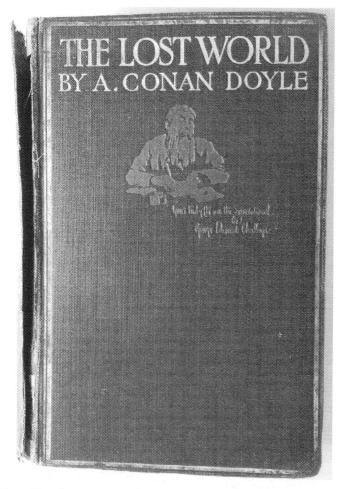

Figure 10 Arthur Conan Doyle, *The Lost World* (Hodder and Stoughton, 1912), front cover – author's personal collection

a strange refraction of observational perspectives – floats a similarly gold-stamped facsimile of the handwritten words that Challenger is, presumably, meant to be writing in this frozen moment: 'Yours truly (to use the conventional lie), George Edward Challenger'. Perhaps the most immediately noticeable feature of this handwriting sample is that it actually appears relatively respectable and neat; in fact, it looks suspiciously unlike the 'barbed-wire' 'scribble' described in Doyle's text. In this, however, there is again a way in which form matches content: if the text of Challenger's epistolary valediction speaks to the deceptive hypocrisies of polite society ('to use the conventional lie'), then the newly civilised neatness with which Challenger has written these public-facing words parodically reinforces this accusation. For, I would argue, much like New Romance more broadly, this front cover is essentially a meditation on themes of theatricality and deception.

The frontispiece to Doyle's novel is a photograph of a homosocial group of friends assuming the roles of Doyle's characters, and there, in the middle of this group of men, sits Doyle himself at a desk with an inkwell, dressed as Professor Challenger. In other words, then, the stylised gold-stamped figure on the novel's front cover is not simply Professor Challenger but a curious hybrid author-character/Doyle-Challenger entity. Above this gold-stamped figure, Doyle's front cover is white-stamped with 'THE LOST WORLD/BY A. CONAN DOYLE'. The subconscious suggestion implicit within this *mise-en-page* repetition of [text] [new line] [author] is that Challenger is just as much the author of this novel as Doyle, and that the novel itself somehow maintains a ghostly subliminal status as a unique aura-infused manuscript relic despite also being an identikit mass-produced print commodity. (Indeed, as if to visually underscore the novel's obsession with multiple playfully complex narrative frames, the cover is itself literally double-framed by a white border.)[21] Ultimately, then, there is a defiant quality to this front cover.

---

[21] Again, there is a symbolic value attached to this choice of colour. Doyle's explorers name the 'lost world' that they discover 'Maple White Land', ostensibly in a chivalric nod to the protagonist's unrequited love interest (i.e., Maple White). Yet the cover's literalisation of this name hints at the polyphonic ways in

While the increasing ubiquity of the typewriter and the spread of modern print culture might have threatened handwriting with extinction (especially by the period in which *The Lost World* was written), as Doyle's explorers discover, sometimes dinosaurs of the past long considered extinct can linger on into the present.

A New Epoch of Artifice

Paradoxically, however, these pointedly anti-modern remnants of handwriting were themselves almost certainly the products of a new, industrial technique. In the early nineteenth century, illustrations were sometimes created using a process known as lithography. An artist would draw directly onto a chemically treated piece of stone, which could then in turn be used to print multiple copies of that image. During this period, lithography remained expensive, and its use in books was therefore severely restricted (Feather, pp. 90–1). This changed, however, in the middle of the nineteenth century, with the invention of 'transfer lithography' – a process that allowed illustrations drawn on specially prepared sheets of paper to then be transferred onto the printing stone. Importantly, John Scally has noted, transfer lithography facilitated lithography's use in steam-powered printing, enabling 'the cheap reproduction of handbills, facsimiles of handwriting, and other small jobs to be done quickly and efficiently' (p. 58).

In 1896, Walter Sickert – an artist whose professional philosophy is sometimes compared with that of William Morris (see, for instance, Baron, p. 2) – condemned transfer lithography as 'a sham':

> the lithographic paper is manufactured to imitate the surface
> of a stone, and the grain is as much a sham as the marbled and
> varnished wall-paper on the staircases in a dear Victorian
> house. The artist who does transfer lithographs is, therefore,
> using a debased instrument. It has its conveniences, it is true,

which the 'white' in 'White Land' can serve as both proper noun and adjective, speaking simultaneously to imperialist notions of blank-sheet *terra nullius* and the naturalisation of white possession.

but it is nonsense to talk of a revival of lithography in these
terms. It is full decadence.

                                    ('Transfer Lithography', pp. 667–8).

Sickert clearly abhorred the mechanical artifice of transfer lithography.[22]
However, a printing technology that used industrially produced simulations
of pre-industrial authenticity (lithographic paper 'manufactured to imitate
the surface of a stone') to produce further industrial simulations of pre-
industrial authenticity (the handwriting facsimiles in these novels) seems
ideally suited to the complex practices and philosophies underpinning the
New Romance movement.

   Yet, as Sickert suggests here, a certain (at times guilty) commitment to
the faux, the mock, the camp, also defined turn-of-the-century society and
culture more broadly. 'Artifice must queen it once more', declared Max
Beerbohm in 1894, going 'full decadence' in the first issue of *The Yellow
Book* – 'The Victorian era comes to its end and . . . the old signs are here . . .
to warn the seer of life that we are ripe for a new epoch of artifice' (p. 65).
And indeed, in his chapter in *The Invention of Tradition*, Hobsbawm singles
out this period in particular as an era of 'profound and rapid social
transformations' that produced a flowering of practices and social groupings
with a synthetic veneer of stabilising history (pp. 263, 303). While
Hobsbawm's chapter is focused on socio-political institutions, the trend
he identifies can also be seen in a range of both middlebrow and elite *fin-de-
siècle* cultural objects and pursuits. Peterson has written of the 'pseudo-
antique' books created by the Manchester-based printing company George
Faulkner and Sons, who – despite famously owning the largest steam
presses in England – featured a hand press in their company logo, and
produced a number of books 'stained both internally and externally to
suggest great age' (pp. 27–8). In architecture, this was an era of not just
'marbled and varnished wall-paper' but the non-load-bearing flying

---

[22] Indeed, seven years earlier (and despite the latter-day comparison noted above),
    Sickert's uncompromising attitude led him to deride Morris and Co. wallpaper as
    the 'endless repetition . . . of adapted patterns, printed by machinery in two or
    three shades of subdued colour' (Sickert, 'Impressionism', p. 59).

buttresses of Gothic Revivalism and the stucco and half-timbering facades of mass-produced Mock Tudor buildings. Composer-ethnographers from Dvořák to Stravinsky to Vaughan Williams tinged their Western art music with sounds, rhythms, and structures they considered reminiscent of their nations' respective folk traditions. Visual artists from Gauguin to Picasso channelled self-consciously 'primitive' and 'naive' influences into their paintings, statues, and collages. In a way, then, New Romance fiction was only one part of a much larger *fin-de-siècle* cultural movement pushing back against the rising tide of modernity.

* * *

At the end of *The Lost World*, one of Doyle's minor characters reflects back on the events and discoveries of the novel, concluding, 'apparently the age of romance [is] not dead' (p. 299). Despite the traditional dominance of progressive linearity within book history and its framing of the Victorian era (a dominance justly critiqued by, amongst others, Michelle Levy and Tom Mole: pp. 102–3), I have argued that the temporal imagination of the New Romance tends to be informed by an epistemology better described as anti-chronological simultaneity. Thus, when these New Romance novels make explicit their intended audience, they typically perform a kind of temporal slippage. As noted above, Stevenson dedicates *Treasure Island* to his fifteen-year-old stepson, 'an American Gentleman'. Two years later, Haggard dedicated *King Solomon's Mines* to 'all the big and little boys who read it'. Even more pointedly, Doyle devotes *The Lost World* to 'the boy who's half a man, Or the man who's half a boy'. The Victorians were intimately familiar with imperialist, socio-Darwinian discourses stretching the stages of man to become the supposed stages of humanity: with dichotomies metaphorically linking children to pre-industrial 'savagery' and adults to modern civilisation (Varty, p. 15). Much like the movement's name itself, the New Romance collapses these binaries to entangle the old within the new and the new within the old.[23]

---

[23] On the prehistoric plateau, Professor Challenger notes in *The Lost World*, 'the old types' can be found 'surviving and living on in company with the newer ones' (p. 252). Professor Challenger is himself provided with a simian doppelgänger in

Andrew Wernick has written of the linguistic shift that took place at the end of the nineteenth century, when the term 'nostalgia' expanded from simply referring to homesickness to meaning both homesickness and a broader longing for the past, 'as if time and place were interchangeable' (p. 219). Whereas *Treasure Island*, *King Solomon's Mines*, and *The Lost World* evoke increasingly ancient temporal settings – those of hidden eighteenth-century treasure, Phoenician Africa, and Mesozoic pre-history – this pre-modern past is never reached through any kind of time travel. Instead, these narratives centre on revealing the 'lost' or 'buried' pre-modern world that remains concealed within the geographic fringes of the modern, and on colonial quests to retrieve remnants of the old to bring back into the present. Indeed, the more expensive 'presentation edition' of Doyle's novel was printed on imitation handmade paper and featured a series of iguanodon footprints sunken into the book's cloth-covered front, back, and spine (see Fig. 11).[24]

As a result, the book itself becomes a kind of ancient archaeological artefact – a hunk of prehistoric earth (pointedly, the vast majority of books in this edition were covered in brown cloth; Green and Gibson, pp. 166–7) both containing and revealing the remains of prehistoric life.

These novels perform a similar kind of exhumation in simulating materio-literary obsolescence. In so doing, New Romance complicates traditional understandings of the nineteenth century's second printing revolution by working against straightforwardly linear models of super-sedence. In this, though, perhaps the genre was not unique. In the decades

---

Doyle's novel, another character describing the chief 'ape-man' they encounter as 'a sort of red Challenger' in appearance (p. 232).

[24] One thousand copies of this edition were printed on thick paper with a mock bevelled edge. Of these, 190 were sold by Hodder and Stoughton, in 1912 (price ten shillings and sixpence). The remaining 810 copies were sold to Henry Frowde, who released them in 1914 (price seven shillings and sixpence). See Green and Gibson, pp. 166–7. One can surmise that this cover design was Doyle's idea, given R. Dana Batory and William A. S. Sarjeant's well-documented claim that *The Lost World* was partly inspired by Doyle's discovery in 1909 of fossilised iguanodon footprints near his house in Sussex (pp. 15–16).

Figure 11 Arthur Conan Doyle, *The Lost World* (Henry Frowde, 1914), front cover of the presentation edition (second issue) – Newberry Library

immediately after movable-type printing arrived in western Europe, scholars such as Anja Grebe and Bernhard Siegert have shown, Flemish and Italian illuminators 'developed a method of giving printed books the appearance of a manuscript', using curling *trompe-l'œil* page corners and other decorative effects to transform incunabula sheets of vellum and paper into pieces of 'simulated three-dimensional architecture' (Grebe, pp. 49–50; Siegert, pp. 177–8). In the twenty-first century, the digitisation of printed books has often produced a similar paradox: a new technology being used to imitate the old technology that it had supposedly made obsolete.

4 New New Romance; or, New Romance 2.0

'The past', declares a minor character in Cressida Cowell's 2009 novel *How to Break a Dragon's Heart*, 'haunts the present in more ways than we realise' (p. 177). Whereas twentieth-century book production largely maintained the nineteenth century's industrial paradigm – as Feather notes, in 'the first half of the twentieth century there was little change', and 'up to about 1985 [change] largely consisted of developing and adopting old ways of doing things' (p. 212) – the late twentieth and early twenty-first centuries produced a moment of rupture in understandings of the book as fundamental as that which had occurred in the mid-to-late Victorian period. 'The physical book's days are numbered', declared a talking head on CNN in 2010, prophesying the death of books within the next five years (Combs). And, indeed, just as the nineteenth-century automation and industrialisation of book production inspired the rearguard nostalgic reaction of Victorian New Romance, so too the perceived epistemological threat of digitisation, I argue, inspired the rearguard nostalgic reaction of New New Romance, or (to employ suitably digitalised language) New Romance 2.0. In many respects, New Romance 2.0 simply echoed Victorian New Romance, producing a series of children's adventure novels, filled with peritextual 'facsimiles' of antique documents and maps, and centred on small groups of explorers searching for ancient worlds 'lost' within the modern. As yet another meta layer of revivalism, however, New New Romance is more extreme and exaggerated than Victorian New Romance. Indeed, I argue in this section, New Romance 2.0 is even more self-conscious, more ironic, and more ambivalent than its Victorian precursor. In the sights of this argument are three lost world series produced between 2003 and 2015 – the period in which anxieties around e-books potentially replacing physical books were at their most acute.[25]

---

[25] After 2015, a popular discourse of media replacement was itself replaced by a discourse of media co-existence. For characteristic examples of the earlier discourse of replacement, see Zeitchik and Reid, Krashinsky, and Davoudi. For characteristic examples of the later co-existence discourse, see Sweney and 'Readers Find Room for Physical and Digital'.

This section focuses on Cressida Cowell's *How to Train Your Dragon* novels (2003–15), Tony DiTerlizzi's *Wondla* trilogy (2010–14), and (to a lesser extent) Tom Taylor's graphic novels *The Deep* (2011–13). Through either their texts or their paratexts, each of these series explicitly relates itself back to turn-of-the-century adventure fiction. Cowell has written of Stevenson's *Treasure Island* map inspiring her to include maps in her novels (Cowell, 'The Wonder of Maps'); the second book in her series is even called *How to Be a Pirate*. At the end of his first *Wondla* novel, DiTerlizzi – originally an illustrator himself – notes the ways in which his highly visual book consciously 'harkens back' to illustrative techniques employed in the late nineteenth and early twentieth centuries (p. 476). The submarine used in *The Deep* is called 'The Arronax', in a knowing wink to Jules Verne's narrator – Professor Aronnax – in *Twenty Thousand Leagues Under the Seas*. Each of these series was created in a different country, and each targeted a subtly different sector of the juvenile fiction market: according to Amazon, Cowell's British series is aimed at those aged between eight and twelve, DiTerlizzi's American trilogy is for those aged ten and above, and Taylor's Australian comic books are for those aged four to eighteen. Despite their differences, however, what these series have in common is both an intense historical awareness and a particular sensitivity to contemporaneous fears that physical books might themselves become 'lost worlds' in the not-too-distant future. Just as Victorian New Romance sought to resist industrial publishing from within industrial publishing, each of these defiantly physical series was also released in a digital format. On each occasion, though, the transition from codex to screen was highly qualified and seemingly reluctant (it took a full decade for e-books of Cowell's series to start appearing, for instance), and these manifestations of anti-digital recalcitrance will be explored further at various moments in this section.

The Book That You Are Holding in Your Hands

While post-millennial anxieties around literary digitisation are routinely recalled today, often with a kind of smug hindsight, perhaps less well remembered is the way in which these anxieties brought with them a renewed awareness of the materiality of physical books as a supposedly dying technology. 'Ebooks have a lot going for them', declared the consumer technology website Engadget, in 2007, but 'it's hard to overcome losing the satisfaction [of] handling a physical book – the texture of the pages, the ability to flip around quickly, and yes, the smell'. 'Other companies might be working on solutions to the harder problems', Engadget explained, 'but ebook content provider CafeScribe is going pretty low-tech to give your laptop screen the same scent as a textbook: the company is shipping "musty smell" scratch-and-sniff stickers with every ebook order' (Patel).

Fears around e-books were heightened further when it came to children, anxieties around a new publishing mode converging with an emerging set of fears about the potential neurological side-effects of childhood 'screen time' more broadly.[26] In 2011, the *New York Times* even published a feature-length article declaring,

> print books may be under siege from the rise of e-books, but they have a tenacious hold on a particular group: children and toddlers [. . . for] parents are insisting this next generation of readers spend their early years with old-fashioned books. This is the case even with parents who themselves are die-hard downloaders of books onto Kindles, iPads, laptops and phones. They freely acknowledge their digital double standard, saying they want their children to be surrounded by print books, to experience turning physical pages as they learn about shapes, colors and animals.
>
> (Richtel and Bosman, B1)

Perhaps as a result, those more formally experimental e-books that did appear for children tended to create curious hybrids of bibliographic and digital materialities (see Henkel, p. 339). Oceanhouse Media's 2015 release

---

[26] A term as seemingly neutral as the 'pure information' of Marshall McLuhan's electric light (McLuhan, p. 60), 'screen time' is, of course, underpinned by a lingering romantic ideology pitting childhood innocence against corrupting modernity.

Alice for the iPad presents Lewis Carroll's story on highly textured facsimiles of worn and yellowed paper, yet it also invites reader-users to employ
the iPad's interactive functionality: on one page, tilting your iPad makes
Alice grow and shrink; on another page, shaking the iPad makes the
characters attending Alice's tea-party shake on screen as well.
Conversely, a decade earlier, Sean Stewart, Jordan Weisman, and Cathy
Brigg released *Cathy's Book*. As its name suggests, *Cathy's Book* is a very
physical codex, replete with the protagonist's hand-drawn doodles and even
an 'evidence pack' filled with torn photographs, a lipstick-stained napkin,
and newspaper clippings that Cathy supposedly discovered during the
course of investigating the fictional mystery; however, the diegesis also
expands out beyond the codex, and readers are encouraged to call function-
ing mock telephone numbers and visit manufactured websites.

It is within this discursive and commercial context, I argue, that we
should view the defiant materiality of print culture in New Romance 2.0,
a genre that returns repeatedly to collections of books and the spatial trope
of the disintegrating library. Thus, both the first and final novels in
DiTerlizzi's *Wondla* trilogy end in the future ruins of the New York
Public Library, an 'ancient building' 'crammed full of tomes from long
ago ... brown decrepit books of every shape and size' (*The Battle for
Wondla*, p. 461; *The Search for Wondla*, p. 452). In a scene that places
a similar emphasis on print culture's antiquated materiality, an increasingly
exasperated character in *The Deep* begins the comic book series by repeatedly grumbling 'We have new maps', as her husband pours over a tattered
ancient chart of historical monster sightings in his private study. 'All sorts of
technology went into' making these new maps, she adds with playful
condescension; 'some of them aren't even drawn in pencil' (pp. 10–11).

Yet perhaps the richest example of the genre's self-conscious obsession
with the materiality of books and the crumbling libraries that contain them
can be found in Cowell's series *How to Train Your Dragon*. As noted above,
it took a full decade for this series to be released in an electronic format, and
even then the first e-book edition of Cowell's series is notable for its
extreme digital minimalism: far from embracing the new medium, Cowell
and her publisher have conspicuously disabled any kind of additional digital
functionality, whether that be the ability to change the text font and size, see

which passages other readers have highlighted, search for dictionary definitions without leaving the Kindle app, or even make digital notes.[27] 'The original book / Now a major motion picture', declares a digital sticker on the front cover of the first e-book edition of the first novel in Cowell's series, and, indeed, there is an element of pro forma box-ticking to this first e-book edition of the series more broadly, as if its release was simply the fulfilment of intercorporate contractual obligations.

For the real obsession of this series is the ageing physicality of the codex. Take, for instance, Cowell's sixth novel, *A Hero's Guide to Deadly Dragons* (2007). In this novel, sequentially the heart of Cowell's series, the adolescent Vikings attempt to steal a book from the 'Meathead Public Library' – a library, we are told, that was 'like a poor neglected fishy Creature who nobody remembers had died in some forgotten corner and was slowly decaying' (p. 82). Discovered by the library's homicidal guardian, 'the Hairy Scary Librarian', one of the children (Fishlegs) frantically flips through the pages of 'a big heavy book called *Swordfighting with Style*' (p. 95), desperately hoping to find some information that might help his friends in the fight that ensues. Cowell's books are heavily illustrated throughout, and the next nine pages are devoted entirely to a remarkable series of full-page illustrations in which we are shown *Swordfighting with Style* from Fishlegs' perspective, Fishlegs' frantic hand movements as he flips through the book rendered in the dynamic visual language of early twentieth-century Futurism.[28]

During this distinctly uncanny textual sequence, when we turn an actual page in Cowell's book our movement is matched by Fishlegs turning a fictional page in his, and Fishlegs' hands merge strangely with our own.

---

[27] Cowell's American publisher, Little, Brown and Co., began releasing the series as e-books in 2013. While Cowell's British publisher, Hodder and Stoughton, released the series with the standard digital functionality, these more elaborate e-books did not begin appearing until 2017.

[28] While copyright restrictions prevent me from reproducing these illustrations here, the relevant pages can, ironically, be viewed in the Internet Archive's digitisation of Cowell's book: https://archive.org/details/herosguideto dead0000cowe_flg5/page/104/mode/2up.

Ultimately, Fishlegs loses patience and, rather than continuing to read the manual as a data-mining textual idealist, he resorts to one final act of desperation. 'He took a good hold of the heavy *Swordfighting with Style* book, and he swung it as hard as he could at the Hairy Scary Librarian's head' (p. 105). ('Well, that's one way to use a book like that', Cowell reflects wryly, in her reading-out-loud YouTube series ('Cressida Reads Book 6', 1:09–1:11), echoing Leah Price in *How to Do Things with Books in Victorian Britain*.) Roger Chartier has written of how e-books turn texts into pure information (pp. 70–2). In this extraordinarily experimental moment, textual ethereality is cast aside in a defiant reassertion of books as fundamentally material objects.

Just as the Hairy Scary Librarian is hit over the head with the self-conscious materiality of physical books, so too the reader (if only figuratively) at the end of *A Hero's Guide to Deadly Dragons*. Through a first-person epilogue, Hiccup (Cowell's protagonist) describes how he subsequently turned the events of the novel into a book, 'the book that you are holding in your hands right now' (p. 190). As if to further underline the point, an accompanying illustration depicts another pair of hands holding another open book, this time a book containing the sentence that we have just read in the text of Cowell's novel.[29]

Splutter and Splotch

As this example from the end of *A Hero's Guide to Deadly Dragons* might suggest, the exaggerated self-consciousness of New Romance 2.0 frequently tips over into a kind of self-parody. Michael Saler has noted that Victorian New Romance was already infused with irony in ways that recent critics tend to either 'underplay or ignore' (p. 71). Yet, whereas the irony of Victorian New Romance is usually fairly subtle, that of New Romance 2.0 is typically quite explicit. Thus, while Haggard enhanced the simulated quality of *King Solomon's Mines* by adding a number of faux ink stains to the map tipped in to its early editions, the first five or six novels in the *How to Train Your Dragon* series stretch this visual discourse to comic excess, each

---

[29] Again, see the Internet Archive's digitisation: https://archive.org/details/herosguidetodead0000cowe_f1g5/page/198/mode/2up.

containing hundreds of ink stains haphazardly strewn throughout the margins of every second or third page. In one sense, these ink stains simply gesture to the fictional manuscript pre-history that Cowell creates for her novels, written retrospectively as they supposedly were with a quill pen by an ageing Hiccup, his unsteady hand causing the ink to 'splutter and splotch when once it ran so smoothly' (*How to Speak Dragonese*, p. 222).[30] However, the sheer number and frequency of these ink stains increasingly encourage Cowell's readers to reflect on their status as highly intentional markers of spontaneous, accidental authenticity: as we are repeatedly reminded, in what becomes the final novel's programmatic refrain, 'accidents happen for a reason' (*How to Fight a Dragon's Fury*, pp. 189, 301).

This ironic self-parody becomes even more explicit in the series' comically flagrant anachronisms. 'Rule Barbarians, Barbarians Rule the Waves', bellow Hiccup's Viking tribe in *How to Twist a Dragon's Tale* (p. 138), before performing a rousing rendition of 'These Bogs Are Your Bogs' a few pages later (p. 147). Moreover, visually, Cowell's novels are littered with 'facsimiles' of Viking writing rendered (by some unexplained magic) not in Norse runes but modern English, and produced in what are clearly late twentieth-century school notebooks and pages torn from spiral notepads.[31] In Section 2, I suggested that Victorian New Romance was defined by an anti-chronological simultaneity in which the ancient lost worlds of dinosaurs and biblical African civilisations could still be found on the fringes of

---

[30] Cowell constructs a full fictional communications circuit around this imagined manuscript pre-history. The series presents itself as Cowell's 'translation' of Hiccup's memoirs, supposedly unearthed in 2002 by 'a boy digging on a beach' who discovered the memoirs covered in a protective 'waterproof dragonskin' (see the prefatory page 'A Note from the Translator' found in first editions of early books in the series). Found-manuscript framing devices such as this were, of course, frequently employed by Victorian New Romance texts (see, for instance, Haggard's 1887 novel *She* and James De Mille's 1888 novel *A Strange Manuscript Found in a Copper Cylinder*).

[31] See, for instance, https://archive.org/details/howtotrainyourdr0000unse_a2a2/page/93/mode/1up?view=theater. See, also, *How to Be a Pirate*, p. 90; *How to Twist a Dragon's Tale*, pp. 88–9, 92–3; *A Hero's Guide to Deadly Dragons*, pp. 41–6; and *How to Break a Dragon's Heart*, pp. 90, 301.

the modern. The lost world adventure novels of New Romance 2.0 take this temporal simultaneity one step further, in an absurdist postmodern reshuffling of historical artefacts and cultural quotations that again foregrounds the materialities of cheap paper production.

While the ironic self-parody of *How to Train Your Dragon* is characterised by a playful impertinence – or, at least the first half of the series can be characterised in this way (the second half of the series shifts increasingly towards the grim pomposity of the later *Harry Potter* novels) – DiTerlizzi's self-parody is a little more reflective in tone. Throughout the *Wondla* trilogy, DiTerlizzi revives a number of key features from Victorian New Romance: the trilogy's basic plot structure revolves around a small band of adventurers searching for a lost world; each novel in the trilogy contains a prominent, intricate map; the final novel ends with a facsimile of a torn and tattered piece of paper (a fragment from the front cover of L. Frank Baum's 1900 novel *The Wonderful Wizard of Oz*, a novel that explicitly inspired the trilogy's title). Halfway through the final book in DiTerlizzi's series, however, we reach a scene that casts an element of doubt over the trilogy's reincarnations. The trilogy is set in a distant future, where an inventor – Cadmus – has sought to create an urban utopia. Now, though, his city is collapsing, and the trilogy's armed protagonist finds the ageing inventor immersed in a holographic vision of the library room of 'an old Victorian-style house' (*The Battle for Wondla*, p. 216). 'This life. This family's love and support is what I wanted to create for my people', Cadmus explains (p. 218). 'You did recreate this perfect life', the inventor's daughter reassures him (p. 219). 'No', DiTerlizzi's protagonist interrupts, shaking her head, before engaging Cadmus in an extended dialogue:

> Cadmus' holographic past was so fully rendered, so tangible, that it was hard for her to dismiss what she was seeing. 'This world, it doesn't exist anymore. It's gone' . . . 'You are wrong', Cadmus now spoke with conviction. 'This world will rise again, I will see it built anew!' [She] fired . . . at the holo-projector. It blew apart in a shower of sparks and shattered holo-bulbs. The emergency lights in the room

activated, bathing all in a bright white light [revealing] cold
gray walls ... 'This, this is reality ... The truth is, that
world you long for in the past was also a dying world'.

(pp. 219–20)

This passage, I would suggest, can best be understood within the framework of the novel's epitextual milieu. Whereas e-books of *How to Train
Your Dragon* and *The Deep* only appeared many years after those series
were first printed, the book and e-book release of DiTerlizzi's *Wondla*
trilogy occurred simultaneously. The first novel in the trilogy even came
with an interactive digital feature that allowed readers to use the printed
book to activate and then navigate an animated, augmented reality
version of the map that it contains, replete with digitised versions of
Meggendorfer-style paper tab-pull figures.[32] In subsequent interviews,
however, DiTerlizzi made it clear that, for him, these digital aspects were
only included out of a somewhat reluctant consequentialism. 'A lot of
kids love technology. And so if there can be a technological aspect that
will get them to pick up the book? Then I'll do it', he told the technology
and culture magazine *Wired*, in 2012. But, he also explained, 'I'm an old-
fashioned person. I could read everything I want on my iPad ... and
I don't. I go and buy the book:

> I'm the guy who still goes and buys CDs, too, and DVDs
> and Blu-Ray discs. I love media and I love having my
> media. And absolutely, with a book, I love the way a book
> feels, and especially a book like WondLa where the pictures
> are so integrated with the text. It's such a big conscious
> design thing that doesn't exist in the e-book version of it.
> That goes full circle back to what we were talking about,
> about the real world versus technology.

(DiTerlizzi and Liu)

---

[32] Though the digital map has since been deactivated, a video of DiTerlizzi demonstrating the digital map can still be viewed on his website: www.wondla.com/home/
wondla-vision-map.

It also seems to go back to *Wondla*'s holograph conversion quoted above, with its pointed critique (and violent destruction) of a digital projector in favour of tangible 'reality'. More than this, though, in these references to a specifically Victorian past – a Victorian past that was itself already 'a dying world' – New Romance 2.0 appears to be struggling to come to terms with its status as a creative movement torn between historicist revivalism and innovation. Indeed, just as Haggard's frontispiece was a transmediated facsimile of a fold-out map, so too the activation of DiTerlizzi's augmented reality map begins with an animated visualisation of a noticeably yellowed map folding open. 'I love a map', DiTerlizzi declared in his interview with *Wired*. '*Peter Pan*, *Winnie the Pooh*, you can go on and on, *Narnia*, *Phantom Tollbooth*, all these books had these amazing maps in them. So what we thought was . . . maybe we can do a 21st-century version of that' (DiTerlizzi and Liu). As *Wondla*'s holograph passage seems to acknowledge, however, this might not be enough. If New Romance 2.0 was to go beyond what Fredric Jameson has called the 'neutral . . . mimicry' of pastiche ('speech in a dead language . . . without any of parody's ulterior motives'; p. 65), it would have to find a way of adding to or subverting the Victorian New Romance genre on which it was constructed.

When Men Were Men and Women Were Sort of Men Too

The most fundamental way in which New Romance 2.0 revises its Victorian precursor is by reimagining the genre's politics. In keeping with its pervasive historical and material nostalgia, Victorian New Romance was (in)famously sympathetic to reactionary ideologies of misogyny and racial supremacy. Indeed, Deane has written of the ways in which Victorian New Romance was essentially underpinned by a convergence of gender-based and colonial chauvinism. In these stories, Deane notes, effeminised modern men typically rediscover an atavistic masculinity of 'raw strength, courage, instinctive violence, bodily size, and homosocial commitment to other men' in the primitive pre-modern worlds they uncover (p. 149).

New New Romance actively works to counteract these now unpalatable (and unmarketable) associations. As is typical of New Romance, *The Deep* involves a group of explorers searching for Atlantis; in this instance, however, Taylor's explorers are a multiracial minority family with an Asian mother and a black father. Rather than a coterie of uber-men, the *Wondla* series revolves around the emotionally supportive family and friends of an adolescent girl. Moreover, rather than maintaining the perspective of the colonisers, *Wondla* – written during a period of growing uncertainty about how long the United States might remain a global superpower – inverts the traditional narrative structures of New Romance, making the series' lost world the future ruins of twenty-first-century New York. As such, a 'Reading Group Guide' question at the end of the first paperback edition of DiTerlizzi's first novel pointedly asks readers to compare the novel's alien invaders with nineteenth-century scientists and colonial explorers such as Lewis and Clark, Audubon, and Darwin – 'greatly admired people who captured "new" creatures, observed them, killed them, and dissected them all in an attempt to understand them' ('Reading Group Guide', p. 485). DiTerlizzi's protagonist even acquires abilities historically associated with Indigenous populations. 'Your species is as ancient as this planet', another character reminds her when she realises she can communicate with animals; 'therefore you may have a connectivity to its denizens' (*A Hero for Wondla*, p. 38). In moments such as these, DiTerlizzi's novels take on the perspective of the colonised (even if, in the process, they also indigenise white America in ways that feel slightly troubling).

Today, one of the most notorious features of Victorian New Romance cartography is a particular detail of the fold-out map that begins *King Solomon's Mines*. In this map, the landscape transforms to take on the appearance of a highly stylised naked African woman (Afro hairstyle and all), in a visual moment that simultaneously sexualises the novel's African setting and objectifies the non-white female body. As if to draw further attention to this aspect of his map, Haggard even provides his readers with a second English-language copy – of what was already a cartographic facsimile – in which this feature of the landscape is highlighted (see Fig. 12).

In *How to Break a Dragon's Heart*, Hiccup tells the reader of how he 'learned that the names on the flat map of the Archipelago . . . were not just made-up fantastical names, but names that related to real people who had real, flesh and blood lives' (p. [i]). However, while Cowell joins Haggard in

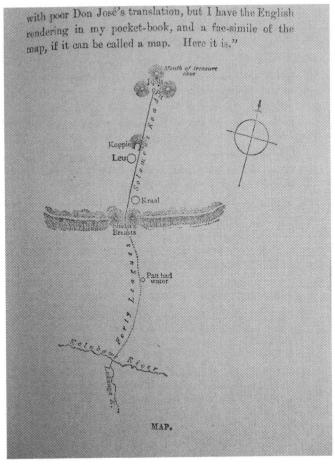

Figure 12 H. Rider Haggard, *King Solomon's Mines* (1885), p. 27 – author's
personal collection

using maps to viscerally humanise the mass-produced books that she creates, she does so through a very different political lens.

In stark contrast to the aggressively-gendered imperialism of Victorian New Romance, Cowell's protagonist returns (perhaps unwittingly) to the Victorian conception of Christian masculinity that Victorian New Romance explicitly rejects, with Hiccup embodying a softer masculinity of intelligence, empathy, compassion, and kindness. Indeed, atavistically brutish masculinity is itself lampooned throughout the series, set as it is in 'a time of VIKING HEROES, in which men were men and women were sort of men too and even some little babies had chest hair' (*How to Speak Dragonese*, p. [iv]). Like DiTerlizzi's trilogy, Cowell's novels take on the perspective of the colonised: 'the Romans', we are told, 'were the Vikings' deadly enemies – a very bossy lot who wanted to take over the world' (*How to Speak Dragonese*, pp. 17–18). Thus, when Cowell includes an anthropomorphic feature on one of her fictional maps – this one, pointedly, a fold-out map, like Haggard's[33] – this feature is noticeably androgenised and de-racialised (*A Hero's Guide to Deadly Dragons*, 2007). Rather than identifiably male or female, black or white, the Isle of the Skullions is simply a skull and crossbones. Linguistically, the 'Isle of the Skullions' references 'Skeleton Island', the island at the heart of Stevenson's novel (in Stevenson's novel, the shape of Skeleton Island is actually described as being like that of 'a fat dragon'; p. 51). Visually, however, this cartographic feature also seems to reinforce Cowell's non-binary message: much like Dickens' rag paper, the skeleton boils down society's distinctions and artificial constructs into an essential human commonality.

[33] This fold-out map can be found in the hardcover first edition of Cowell's novel.

Conclusion

At the end of the 1990s, Eliza Dresang argued that children's literature was undergoing a process of 'Radical Change'. Text and image were starting to blur; readers were increasingly being invited to engage with books in interesting physical ways; the use of multiple narrative and visual frames was becoming more and more common. For Dresang, these changes suggested that printed books for children were beginning to borrow forms from the digital realm: that printed books were coming to resemble the Internet. For me, however, these changes suggest that, faced with the Internet, books (at least, the ones that interest me) were rediscovering the potential of the codex and exploring the various text technologies that made books distinct from other kinds of media. In short, I suggest, books were becoming more like books.

In part, this interpretive divergence may simply be the result of the different periods in which Dresang was, and I am, writing – Dresang in a moment of great boosterism about the Internet and its transformative potential, I in a moment of increasing concern about the effects of the Internet on people and the societies in which they live. As is often noted, the early decades of the twenty-first century – with their growing awareness of inequalities and their general sense of economic, geopolitical, and bio-pathogenic crisis – bear an increasingly uncanny resemblance to the *fin-de-siècle* and all of that era's anxieties about what the future might contain. With those anxieties today has come a noticeable media turn towards the comforting invented tradition of the remake and the sequel, whether various recent Disney films, steampunk neo-Victorianism, reprisals of *Jumanji*, or (in a particularly curious instance of nostalgia for nostalgia) the 2021 series *The Wonder Years*. The same kind of nostalgic media return characterised, I have argued, late Victorian lost world adventure fiction. Within this nostalgic paradigm, content and media form intertwine: the obsolete text technologies being recreated become as much the focus as the diegetic world that these media forms are ostensibly being used to represent. It seems fitting for these processes to converge on lost world adventure fiction, specifically – a genre animated by modernity's multiple concomitant timeframes, a blurring of the juvenile and the adult, and a sense that the dinosaurs of materiality might linger on in the simulated present.

A Chronology of Events Discussed in This Element

1798:	The Fourdrinier papermaking machine invented in Paris.
1803:	The first commercial Fourdrinier machine installed in Frogmore, England.
1814:	*The Times* newspaper becomes the first mass-circulation document printed on a steam-powered printing machine.
1824:	Total quantity of machine-made paper in Britain eclipses that of handmade paper.
1825:	A patent is granted to John and Christopher Phipps for the dandy roll (a device used to give machine-made paper the appearance of handmade paper).
1865:	H. W. Lord reports that, in Britain, 'the bulk of printed matter' is now printed on a steam press.
1873:	Esparto grass overtakes rag as the key component of paper in Britain.
1881 (August):	Robert Louis Stevenson begins writing *Treasure Island*.
1881 (October):	*Treasure Island; or, The Mutiny of the Hispaniola* begins appearing as a serial in the children's magazine *Young Folks*.
1881 (October):	Stevenson travels with his wife (Fanny) and stepson (Lloyd) to Davos, Switzerland. Stevenson begins experimenting with Lloyd's miniature hand-operated printing press.
1881 (November):	Stevenson completes *Treasure Island*.
1882 (January):	The serialisation of *Treasure Island* in *Young Folks* completed. Stevenson is paid a total of £37 7s 6d for the serial.

1883 (May):	Cassell & Company offer to publish *Treasure Island* as a book. Stevenson to be paid £100 for the first 4,000 copies and a further £20 for every additional 1,000 copies sold in Britain.
1883 (November):	Publication of the first book edition of *Treasure Island* by Cassell & Company, price five shillings. 12,000 copies sold by 1886.
1885:	Frederick Wilson claims that 'nearly every printing-office' in Britain now possesses a steam-powered printing press.
1885 (January):	H. Rider Haggard begins writing *King Solomon's Mines*.
1885 (April):	Haggard finishes writing *King Solomon's Mines*.
1885 (September):	*King Solomon's Mines* first published by Cassell & Company, price five shillings. 31,000 copies sold within one year. Haggard to be paid on a royalty basis.
1893:	Wood pulp overtakes esparto as the key component of paper in Britain.
1912 (April):	*The Lost World* begins its serialisation in the *Strand*.
1912 (October):	First book edition of *The Lost World* published by Hodder and Stoughton, price six shillings. Around 11,000 copies printed upon first release. An additional 1,000 copies of a 'presentation edition' printed, though only 190 bound and sold (price ten shillings and sixpence).
1912 (November):	*The Lost World* serialisation concludes.
1914:	The remaining 810 copies of *The Lost World*'s presentation edition bound and sold (price seven shillings and sixpence).
1971:	Project Gutenberg founded.
1998:	Release of the first commercial e-book reader, the Rocket.
2003:	Cressida Cowell publishes the first book in her series, *How to Train Your Dragon*. The novel will

	sell more than three million copies in the next ten years.
2007:	Amazon release their first Kindle.
2010:	Tony DiTerlizzi's *The Search for Wondla* published by Simon and Schuster as a codex and an e-book.
2011:	Publication of the first instalment of Tom Taylor's comic book series *The Deep*.
2012:	Amazon sells more e-books than print books.
2012:	*A Hero for Wondla* published as a codex and an e-book.
2013:	The final instalment of *The Deep* is published.
2013 (December):	*How to Train Your Dragon* first released as an e-book.
2014:	*The Battle for Wondla* published as a codex and an e-book.
2015:	Cowell publishes the last book in her *How to Train Your Dragon* series.
2016:	*The Deep* first published as an e-book.

References

Abate, Michelle Ann. *No Kids Allowed: Children's Literature for Adults*. Baltimore, MD: Johns Hopkins University Press, 2020.

'An Act to Establish a Register of Trade Marks', pp. 1–5, in *Bills, Public: Volume VI, Session 5 February–13 August 1875 (Railway Companies to Statute Law Revision)*. London: The House of Commons, 1875.

'Aunt Louisa's Toy Books' (advertisement). *The Athenaeum: Journal of English and Foreign Literature, Science, the Fine Arts, Music and the Drama* 2762 (2 October 1880): p. 421.

Batory, R. Dana, and Sarjeant, William A. S. 'Sussex Iguanadon Footprints and the Writing of the Lost World', pp. 13–18, in David D. Gillette and Martin G. Lockley, eds., *Dinosaur Tracks and Traces*. Cambridge: Cambridge University Press, 1991.

Baudrillard, Jean. *Simulacra and Simulation*. Translated by Sheila Faria Glaser. Ann Arbor: University of Michigan Press, 1994.

Baughan, Rosa. *Character Indicated by Handwriting*. London: 'The Bazaar' Office, [1880].

Beerbohm, Max. 'A Defence of Cosmetics'. *The Yellow Book: An Illustrated Quarterly* 1.1 (April 1894): pp. 65–82.

Bentley, Lionel. *Trade Marks and Brands: An Interdisciplinary Critique*. Cambridge: Cambridge University Press, 2008.

Berman, Marshall. *All That Is Solid Melts into Air: The Experience of Modernity*. New York: Simon and Schuster, 1982.

Blackburn, Henry. *The Art of Illustration*. London: W. H. Allen, 1894.

Bonnett, Alastair. *The Geography of Nostalgia: Global and Local Perspectives on Modernity and Loss*. London: Routledge, 2016.

Boyd, Kelly. *Manliness and the Boys' Story Paper in Britain: A Cultural History, 1855–1940*. Basingstoke: Palgrave, 2003.

Brantlinger, Patrick. *Rule of Darkness: British Literature and Imperialism, 1830–1914.* Ithaca, NY: Cornell University Press, 2013.

Bristow, Joseph. *Empire Boys: Adventures in a Man's World.* London: Routledge, 1991.

Burnett, Frances Hodgson. 'The Drury Lane Boys' Club: What It Grew from, What It Is, and What We Hope It Will Be'. *Scribner's Magazine* 11.6 (June 1892): pp. 676–90.

Bushell, Sally. 'Mapping Victorian Adventure Fiction: Silences, Doublings, and the Ur-Map in *Treasure Island* and *King Solomon's Mines*'. *Victorian Studies* 57.4 (July 2015): pp. 611–37.

'The Calli-Graphic Pen' (advertisement). *The Critic & Good Literature* 4.2 (19 January 1884): p. iv.

Carr, John Dickson. *The Life of Arthur Conan Doyle.* London: John Murray, 1949.

'Catalogue of Toy Books' (advertisement), pp. 25–8, in *Tales of Fairy Land.* London: Routledge, 1879.

Chartier, Roger. *The Author's Hand and the Printer's Mind.* Translated by Lydia G. Cochrane. Cambridge: Polity Press, 2014.

Clair, Colin. *A History of European Printing.* London: Academic Press, 1976.

Combs, Cody. 'Will Physical Books Be Gone in Five Years?' *CNN*, 18 October 2010. www.cnn.com/2010/TECH/innovation/10/17/negroponte.ebooks/index.html (accessed 23 October 2021).

Cowell, Cressida. 'Cressida Reads Book 6: A Hero's Guide to Deadly Dragons: Last Part Chapter 9 of A Hero's Guide'. *YouTube*, 28 August 2020. www.youtube.com/watch?v=t6eXHXahoX4&list=PLBHPLU9xAmxe-3xrDoUU14G1PPhvXihqT&index=12 (accessed 18 August 2021).

  A Hero's Guide to Deadly Dragons. London: Hodder Children's Books, 2007.

  How to Be a Pirate. London: Hodder Children's Books, 2004.

  How to Break a Dragon's Heart. London: Hodder Children's Books, 2009.

How to Fight a Dragon's Fury. New York: Little, Brown and Company, 2015.

How to Speak Dragonese. New York: Little, Brown and Company, 2006.

How to Train Your Dragon. London: Hodder Children's Books, 2003.

How to Twist a Dragon's Tale. London: Hodder Children's Books, 2007.

'The Wonder of Maps'. *BookTrust*, 20 December 2016. www.booktrust .org.uk/news-and-features/features/2016/december/the-wonder-of-maps/ (accessed 14 January 2022).

'Currency Converter: 1270–2017'. *The National Archives*. www.nationalarc hives.gov.uk/currency-converter (accessed 8 October 8 2021).

Davoudi, Salamander. 'Bloomsbury's Ebook Sales Increase 70% Year on Year'. *Financial Times*, 12 July 2012: p. 18.

Deane, Bradley. *Masculinity and the New Imperialism: Rewriting Manhood in British Popular Literature, 1870–1914*. Cambridge: Cambridge University Press, 2014.

'Death of Mr. Walter'. *The Times*, 29 July 1847: p. 7.

[Dickens, Charles, and Lemon, Mark]. 'A Paper-Mill'. *Household Words* 1.23 (31 August 1850): pp. 529–31.

DiTerlizzi, Tony. *The Battle for Wondla*. New York: Simon and Schuster, 2014.

A Hero for Wondla. New York: Simon and Schuster, 2012.

The Search for Wondla. New York: Simon and Schuster, 2010.

DiTerlizzi, Tony, and Liu, Jonathan H. 'GeekDad Interview: Author-Illustrator Tony DiTerlizzi'. *Wired*, 10 May 2012. www.wired.com/2012/tony-diterlizzi-interview (accessed 11 October 2021).

Doyle, Arthur Conan. *The Lost World: Being an Account of the Recent Amazing Adventures of Professor George E. Challenger, Lord John Roxton, Professor Sumerlee, and Mr. E. D. Malone of the 'Daily Gazette'*. London: Hodder and Stoughton, 1912.

'The Lost World: Chapter XV (Continued)'. *The Strand Magazine* 44.263 (November 1912): pp. 483–96.

'The Sign of the Four'. *Lippincott's Monthly Magazine* 45.2 (February 1890): pp. 147–223.

Dresang, Eliza T. *Radical Change: Books for Youth in a Digital Age*. New York: The H. W. Wilson Company, 1999.

Durkin, Philip. 'When Is a Book a Tree?' *OUPblog*, 15 June 2004. https://blog.oup.com/2014/06/origin-word-book-etymology/ (accessed 20 July 2021).

'Effect of the Electric Light upon Books'. *English Mechanic and World of Science*, 22 July 1887: p. 483.

Ehland, Christoph, and Gohrisch, Jana, eds. *Imperial Middlebrow*. Leiden: Brill, 2020.

Feather, John. *A History of British Publishing*. New York: Routledge, 2006.

Fernandez, Jean. *Geography and the Literary Imagination in Victorian Fictions of Empire: The Politics of Imperial Space*. New York: Routledge, 2020.

Frith, Henry. *Guide to the Study of Graphology: With an Explanation of Some of the Mysteries of Handwriting*. London: Routledge, 1886.

Fyfe, Aileen. *Steam-Powered Knowledge: William Chambers and the Business of Publishing, 1820–1860*. Chicago: University of Chicago Press, 2012.

Garside, Peter. 'Literature in the Marketplace: The Rise of the Scottish Literary Market', pp. 203–77, in Bill Bell, ed., *The Edinburgh History of the Book in Scotland: Volume 3 (Industry and Ambition, 1800–80)*. Edinburgh: Edinburgh University Press, 2007.

Grebe, Anja. 'Frames and Illusion: The Function of Borders in Late Medieval Book Illumination', pp. 43–69, in Werner Wolf and Walter Bernhart, eds., *Framing Borders in Literature and Other Media*. Amsterdam: Rodopi, 2006.

Green, Richard Lancelyn, and Gibson, John Michael. *A Bibliography of A. Conan Doyle*. Oxford: Oxford University Press, 1983.

Haggard, H. Rider. 'About Fiction'. *The Contemporary Review* 51.2 (February 1887): pp. 172–80.

   The Days of My Life. An Autobiography in Two Volumes: Volume I. London: Longmans, Green and Co., 1926.

   King Solomon's Mines. London: Cassell & Company, 1885.

   'The Three-Volume Novel: To the Editor of the Times'. *The Times*, 27 July 1894: p. 11.

Hampson, Robert. 'A Note on the Text', pp. 44–9, in *King Solomon's Mines*. London: Penguin, 2007.

Hart, James D. *The Private Press Ventures of Samuel Lloyd Osbourne and R. L. S. with Facsimiles of Their Publications*. San Francisco: The Book Club of California, 1966.

[Hazlitt, William]. 'The Periodical Press: Art. IV'. *The Edinburgh Review* 38.3 (May 1823): pp. 349–78.

   'Theatrical Examiner. No. 240'. *Examiner*, 17 June 1816: pp. 378–9.

Henkel, Ayoe Quist. 'Exploring the Materiality of Literary Apps for Children'. *Children's Literature in Education* 49.3 (September 2018): pp. 338–55.

Henley, W. E. 'Unsigned Review [in] "Saturday Review", 8 December 1883', pp. 131–6, in Paul Maixner, ed., *Robert Louis Stevenson: The Critical Heritage*. London: Routledge, 1998.

Hobsbawm, Eric. 'Mass-Producing Traditions: Europe, 1870–1914', pp. 263–308, in Eric Hobsbawm and Terence Ranger, eds., *The Invention of Tradition*. Cambridge: Cambridge University Press, 1983.

How, Harry. 'Illustrated Interviews. No. VII. – Mr. H. Rider Haggard'. *The Strand Magazine: An Illustrated Monthly* 3.1 (January 1892): pp. 3–17.

Howitt, William. *Cassell's Illustrated History of England During the Last Hundred Years: Volume V.* London: Cassell, Petter, and Galpin, 1861.

'The Ideal Writing Machine: The Caligraph' (advertisement). *The Critic & Good Literature* 4.2 (19 January 1884): p. iv.

Jameson, Fredric. 'Postmodernism, or the Cultural Logic of Late Capitalism'. *New Left Review* 146 (July/August 1984): pp. 53–92.

Japp, Alexander H. *Robert Louis Stevenson: A Record, An Estimate, and a Memorial.* New York: Charles Scribner's Sons, 1905.

Katz, Wendy R. *Rider Haggard and the Fiction of Empire: A Critical Study of British Imperial Fiction.* Cambridge: Cambridge University Press, 1987.

Kestner, Joseph A. *Masculinities in British Adventure Fiction, 1880–1915.* New York: Routledge, 2010.

'King Solomon's Mines. A Thrilling Tale Founded on an African Legend' (advertisement). *Morning Post*, 19 October 1885: p. 1.

Koehler, Karin. 'Judging by the Hand, Handwriting and Character in Victorian Literary Culture', pp. 220–40, in James Gregory, Daniel J. R. Grey, and Annika Bautz, eds., *Judgement in the Victorian Age.* London: Routledge, 2019.

Krashinsky, Susan. 'Amazon E-book Sales Surpass Paper'. *Globe and Mail*, 20 May 2011: p. B9.

Lellenberg, Jon, Stashower, Daniel, and Foley, Charles. *Arthur Conan Doyle: A Life in Letters.* New York: Penguin, 2007.

Levy, Michelle and Mole, Tom. *The Broadview Introduction to Book History.* Peterborough, Canada: Broadview, 2017.

'The Literary Field'. *Cleveland Daily Herald*, 17 February 1884: p. 10.

Littau, Karin. *Theories of Reading: Books, Bodies, and Bibliomania.* Cambridge: Polity, 2006.

Lloyd, John Uri. *Etidorhpa, or, the End of Earth.* Cincinnati: The Robert Clarke Company, 1896.

'London, Wednesday, July 25, 1894'. *The Times*, 25 July 1894: pp. 9–10.

Lord, H. W. 'Report on Printers, Bookbinders, Stationers, &c.' in *Children's Employment Commission (1862): Fifth Report of the Commissioners. Presented to Both Houses of Parliament by Command of Her Majesty*. London: Her Majesty's Stationery Office, 1866.

Magee, Gary Bryan. *Productivity and Performance in the Paper Industry: Labour, Capital, and Technology in Britain and America, 1860–1914*. Cambridge: Cambridge University Press, 1997.

Marx, Karl. *Capital: A Critical Analysis of Capitalist Production*. Translated by Samuel Moore and Edward Aveling. London: Swan Sonnenschein, Lowry, & Co., 1887.

Mathison, Ymitri. 'Maps, Pirates and Treasure: The Commodification of Imperialism in Nineteenth-Century Boys' Adventure Fiction', pp. 173–85, in Dennis Denisoff, ed., *The Nineteenth-Century Child and Consumer Culture*. Aldershot: Ashgate, 2008.

McLuhan, Marshall. *Understanding Media: The Extensions of Man*. New York: McGraw-Hill, 1964.

Menke, Richard. 'New Grub Street's Ecologies of Paper'. *Victorian Studies* 61.1 (October 2018): pp. 60–82.

Miller, Elizabeth Carolyn. *Slow Print: Literary Radicalism and Late Victorian Print Culture*. Stanford, CA: Stanford University Press, 2013.

Morris, William. 'The Ideal Book', pp. 179–86, in *Transactions of the Bibliographical Society, Session 1892–3*. London: The Bibliographic Society, 1893.

'Mr. William Morris's Kelmscott Press Publications' (advertisement). *The Morning Post*, 14 October 1896: p. 8.

'The New Patent Novel Writer'. *Punch, or the London Charivari*, 14 December 1844: p. 268.

'Notices of Books: The Art of Paper-Making'. *The Chemical News and Journal of Physical Science*, 9 May 1890: p. 226.

Osbourne, Lloyd. 'Note by Lloyd Osbourne', pp. ix–xi, in *Treasure Island. Prince Otto*. New York: Heinemann, 1922.

'Our Letter Box'. *Young Folks: A Boys' and Girls' Paper of Instructive and Entertaining Literature* 19.571 (12 November 1881): p. 7.

'Our Letter Box'. *Young Folks: A Boys' and Girls' Paper of Instructive and Entertaining Literature* 19.572 (19 November 1881): p. 7.

Patel, Nilay. 'CafeScribe Gives Ebook Readers Musty Smell of the Real Things'. *Engadget*, 24 August 2007. www.engadget.com/2007-08-24-cafescribe-gives-ebook-readers-musty-smell-of-the-real-thing.html (accessed 16 June 2021).

Peterson, William S. *The Kelmscott Press: A History of William Morris's Typographical Adventure*. Berkeley: The University of California Press, 1991.

Pinto, Edward H. *Treen: Or, Small Woodware Through the Ages*. London: B. T. Batsford, 1949.

Rains, Stephanie. 'Reading the Hand: Palmistry, Graphology and Alternatives Literacies', pp. 176–90, in Rebecca Anne Barr, Sarah-Anne Buckley, and Muireann O'Cinneide, eds., *Literacy, Language and Reading in Nineteenth-Century Ireland*. Liverpool: Liverpool University Press, 2019.

Raven, James. 'The Book Trades', pp. 1–34, in Isabel Rivers, ed., *Books and Their Readers in Eighteenth-Century England: New Essays*. London: Continuum, 2001.

'Readers Find Room for Physical and Digital'. *The Dominion Post* (Wellington, NZ), 17 May 2017: p. 5.

'Reading Group Guide', pp. 484–6, in *The Search for Wondla*. New York: Simon and Schuster, 2012.

Richards, Jeffrey, ed. *Imperialism and Juvenile Literature*. Manchester: Manchester University Press, 1989.

Richtel, Matt, and Bosman, Julie. 'To Serve the Young, E-Book Fans Prefer Print'. *New York Times*, 21 November 2011: pp. B. 1, B. 9.

'A Romance of the Buccaneers'. *The Guernsey Star*, 22 December 1883: p. 4.

Saler, Michael. *As If: Modern Enchantment and the Literary Prehistory of Virtual Reality*. Oxford: Oxford University Press, 2012.

Scally, John. 'Illustration', pp. 49–64, in Bill Bell, ed., *The Edinburgh History of the Book in Scotland*. Edinburgh: Edinburgh University Press, 2007.

Scott, Sir Walter. *Tales of the Crusaders, in Four Volumes: Volume I (The Betrothed)*. Edinburgh: Archibold, Constable and Co., 1825.

'The Selection of Paper'. *The American Bookmaker: A Journal of Technical Art and Information* 10.1 (January 1890): p. 4.

Senchyne, Jonathan. *The Intimacy of Paper in Early and Nineteenth-Century American Literature*. Amherst: University of Massachusetts Press, 2020.

Sickert, Walter. 'Impressionism', pp. 59–61, in Anna Gruetzner Robins, ed., *Walter Sickert: The Complete Writings on Art*. Oxford: Oxford University Press, 2003.

   'Transfer Lithography', *Saturday Review* 82.2148 (26 December 1896): pp. 667–8.

Siegert, Bernhard. *Cultural Techniques: Grids, Filters, Doors, and Other Articulations of the Real*. Translated by Geoffry Winthrop-Young. New York: Fordham University Press, 2015.

Southward, John. *Progress in Printing and the Graphic Arts During the Victorian Era*. London: Simpkin, Marshall, Hamilton, Kent & Co., 1897; Cambridge: Cambridge University Press, 2012.

Spooner, W. A. 'Handwriting and Character'. *Murray's Magazine* 4.23 (November 1888): pp. 656–65.

Spicer, A. Dykes. *The Paper Trade: A Descriptive and Historical Survey of the Paper Trade from the Commencement of the Nineteenth Century*. London: Methuen, 1907.

Starre, Alexander. 'The Pleasures of Paper: Tethering Literature to Obsolete Material Form', pp.127–44, in Babette B. Tischleder and

Sarah Wasserman, eds., *Cultures of Obsolescence: History, Materiality, and the Digital Age*. New York: Palgrave Macmillan, 2015.

Stevenson, Robert Louis. 'To W. E. Henley (August 1881)', pp. 257–9, in Sidney Colvin, ed., *The Letters of Robert Louis Stevenson to His Family and Friends: Volume I*. New York: Charles Scribner's Sons, 1899.

  Treasure Island. London: Cassell & Company, 1883.

  Strange Case of Dr Jekyll and Mr Hyde. London: Longmans, Green, and Co., 1886.

  'My First Book – "Treasure Island"'. *The Idler Magazine: An Illustrated Monthly* 6.1 (August 1894): pp. 3–11.

Stevenson, Robert Louis, and Osbourne, Samuel Lloyd. *Not I, and Other Poems*. Davos, Switzerland: S. L. Osbourne & Company, 1881. https://digital.nls.uk/99384416 (accessed 19 June 2021).

The Story of the House of Cassell. London: Cassell & Company, 1922.

Sweney, Mark. 'Printed Book Sales Rise for First Time in Four Years as Ebooks Decline'. *The Guardian*, 13 May 2016. www.theguardian.com/media/2016/may/13/printed-book-sales-ebooks-decline (accessed 26 July 2021).

Taylor, Tom. *The Deep: Here Be Dragons #1*. Applecross, WA: Gestalt, 2011.

Thomas, William. *Diary, 1914–15*. National Library of Wales, Aberystwth, GB 0210 WILMAS. www.open.ac.uk/Arts/reading/UK/record_details.php?id=32167 (accessed 15 October 2021).

Thornton, Tamara Plakins. *Handwriting in America: A Cultural History*. New Haven, CT: Yale University Press, 1996.

'Treasure Island. A Story of the Spanish Main' (advertisement). *The Pall Mall Gazette*, 20 November 1883: p. 16.

'The Type Writer'. *The Times*, 25 April 1876: p. 6.

'The Type Writer' (advertisement). *Sheffield Independent*, 6 June 1876: p. 1.

Varty, Anne. *Children and Theatre in Victorian Britain*. Houndmills, Basingstoke: Palgrave Macmillan, 2008.

Vranken, Thomas. *Literary Experiments in Magazine Publishing: Beyond Serialisation*. London: Routledge, 2020.

Wall, Barbara. *The Narrator's Voice: The Dilemma of Children's Fiction*. New York: St. Martin's Press, 1991.

[Walter, John]. 'London, Tuesday, November 29, 1814'. *The Times*, 29 November 1814: p. 3.

Webb, Sidney, and Webb, Beatrice. *Industrial Democracy: Volume One*. London: Longmans, Green, and Co., 1897.

Wernick, Andrew. 'Resort to Nostalgia: Mountains, Memories and Myths of Time', pp. 207–23, in Mica Nava, Andrew Blake, Iain MacRury, and Barry Richards, eds., *Buy this Book: Studies in Advertising and Consumption*. London: Routledge, 1997.

Whalley, Joyce Irene. *Cobwebs to Catch Flies: Illustrated Books for the Nursery and Schoolroom, 1700–1900*. Berkeley: University of California Press, 1975.

'Why Does Paper Turn Yellow?' *Chamber's Journal of Popular Literature, Science, and Art* 4.176 (14 May 1887): p. 320.

Wilson, Frederick J. F. *Typographic Printing Machines and Machine Printing. A Practical Guide to the Selection of Bookwork, Two-Colour, Jobbing and Rotary Machines. With Remarks Upon their Construction, Capabilities, and Peculiarities*. London: Wyman and Sons, 1879.

Wood, H. Trueman. *Modern Methods of Illustrating Books*. London: Elliot Stock, 1887.

'Writing Superseded'. *The Flintshire Observer* (Flintshire, Wales), 7 January 1876: p. 2.

Wynne, Deborah. 'Reading Victorian Rags: Recycling, Redemption, and Dickens's Ragged Children'. *Journal of Victorian Culture* 20.1 (January 2015): pp. 34–49.

Zeitchik, Steven and Reid, Calvin. 'January E-book Sales Show Surprising Strength'. *Publisher's Weekly* 250.13 (31 March 2003): p. 12.

Acknowledgements

While this Element may be short, its existence is testament to the expertise and generosity of a lengthy list of people. First and foremost, thanks go to Eugene Giddens, for all of his insights and constructive suggestions, and for his good-humoured professionalism in ensuring that the production of this Element went so smoothly. I am also grateful to the Element's two blind peer-reviewers, for their helpful suggestions and words of support. I began ruminating on these ideas when I first encountered Michael Saler's wonderful book *As If* almost ten years ago. Two of the great thrills of my academic career so far were (firstly) when Michael agreed to read an earlier draft of this material and (secondly) when he then proved enthusiastic about and receptive to the new direction in which I had taken his original findings. Earlier versions of this Element were also read by Suzy Anger, Tom Mole, and Julian Thomas, and I thank each of them for their tremendously useful expert feedback and support. In 2020, I presented part of this material in the online seminar series 'Seeing Double: Books, Narratives, and Virtual Realities', hosted by the Enlightenment, Romanticism, and Contemporary Culture Research Unit at the University of Melbourne. My thanks go to the always brilliant Clara Tuite, for inviting me to speak in this series, and to all of the people who attended the session and participated in the discussion.

This Element is partly the product of various fleeting and serendipitous encounters. Thanks go to Justin Clemens, who stopped me in the halls of the University of Melbourne's John Medley Building to show me Bernhard Siegert's work on transmedia frames. During a flying visit to the UK, in the lost world that was 2019, Simon Schaffer and John Tresch very generously agreed to meet with me – an unknown postdoctoral scholar – for what proved to be highly stimulating discussions about authorship and mechanisation in the nineteenth century. Thanks go to the various libraries who provided me with the images in this Element, and especially to Heather Dean (Associate Director of Special Collections at the University of Victoria) who arranged for me to be given a scan of Figure 6 on a pro bono basis. Finally, at CUP, I thank commissioning editor Bethany Thomas and series editors Samantha Rayner and Leah Tether for supporting the inclusion of this Element in their series.

Cambridge Elements ≡

Publishing and Book Culture

SERIES EDITOR
Samantha Rayner
University College London

Samantha Rayner is Professor of Publishing and Book Cultures at UCL. She is also Director of UCL's Centre for Publishing, co-Director of the Bloomsbury CHAPTER (Communication History, Authorship, Publishing, Textual Editing and Reading) and co-Chair of the Bookselling Research Network.

ASSOCIATE EDITOR
Leah Tether
University of Bristol

Leah Tether is Professor of Medieval Literature and Publishing at the University of Bristol. With an academic background in medieval French and English literature and a professional background in trade publishing, Leah has combined her expertise and developed an international research profile in book and publishing history from manuscript to digital.

ABOUT THE SERIES

This series aims to fill the demand for easily accessible, quality texts available for teaching and research in the diverse and dynamic fields of Publishing and Book Culture. Rigorously researched and peer-reviewed Elements will be published under themes, or 'Gatherings'. These Elements should be the first check point for researchers or students working on that area of publishing and book trade history and practice: we hope that, situated so logically at Cambridge University Press, where academic publishing in the UK began, it will develop to create an unrivalled space where these histories and practices can be investigated and preserved.

Cambridge Elements ☰

Publishing and Book Culture

Children's Publishing

Gathering Editor: Eugene Giddens

Eugene Giddens is Skinner-Young Professor of Shakespeare and
Renaissance Literature at Anglia Ruskin University. His work
considers the history of the book from the early modern period
to the present. He is co-author of *Lewis Carroll's* Alice's
Adventures in Wonderland *and* Through the Looking-Glass*:*
A Publishing History (2013).

ELEMENTS IN THE GATHERING

Picture-Book Professors: Academia and Children's Literature
Melissa Terras

Christmas Books for Children
Eugene Giddens

The Rise of American Girls' Literature
Ashley N. Reese

Simulating Antiquity in Boys' Adventure Fiction: Maps and Ink Stains
Thomas Vranken

A full series listing is available at: www.cambridge.org/EPBC

Printed in the United States
by Baker & Taylor Publisher Services